Missing Music

Missing Music

Voices from Where the Dirt Roads End

Ian Brennan

Foreword by Dame Evelyn Glennie
Photos by Marilena Umuhoza Delli

ISBN: 979-8-88744-037-8 (paperback)
ISBN: 979-8-88744-047-7 (ebook)
Library of Congress Control Number: 2023944311
Cover by John Yates / www.stealworks.com
Interior design by briandesign

10 9 8 7 6 5 4 3 2 1

PM Press
PO Box 23912
Oakland, CA 94623
www.pmpress.org

Printed in the USA.

Contents

NOTE FROM THE AUTHOR

This is not intended to be an academic book.

Should I ever write the words "subaltern" or "libidinal" in my lifetime, I expect to rightly be imprisoned for crimes against humanity.

My goal remains impressions rather than authoritative dispatch. This book focuses on narratives, leaving the didactic material on the side (that is, *mostly*).

Have the courage to make love in the light,
but sing in the dark.
For no external reward, other than the moment.
Just for the fuck of it.

FOREWORD

To draw upon the belief of the highly influential American musical figure Harry Partch that the individual's path "cannot be retraced, because each of us is an original human being" brings forth the observation that any creative endeavor is indeed a journey rather than a destination. Music is as complex, inexplicable, and unknowable as those who participate in it. What does "participation" actually mean when dealing with this kind of fluid art form? Who are the participators, the decision-makers? How have our lives, charged with the tsunami of social media outlets and expression, changed our relationship with an art form that is currently becoming less about patience or physical sensation and instead about what is in vogue, what is "good," what we "should" be digesting in our lives?

I am a sound creator. All my senses interact with sound because it is the brain that acts as the conductor—tying and redirecting the myriad of emotions connected with sound. Ultimately, the brain redefines how we have thought to have understood our senses.

Some common questions I am asked are: What has been my most "successful" concert? What has been the "high point" of my career so far? What was the event where I knew I was "successful"? All of these make me feel a tad uncomfortable because I don't feel any more successful than on the first day I picked up a pair of sticks. Of course, I feel I am a better and more refined musician now but that doesn't constitute success. I don't feel any more successful since making my first solo recording versus my fortieth or winning a school swimming badge in comparison to winning a Grammy. "Success" is not a word I relate to, because becoming better at something is a never-ending, patient journey. I am constantly weeding my sound garden and trying to become a better percussionist and musician. If I had to define "success" it would be the heightened curiosity I have been able to sustain, the wonderment in seeing a street performer or a baby handling a rattle for the first time or witnessing the great orchestras of the world or the local pub folk group. I love it all. Not necessarily because I like or dislike the music but because it touches an emotion within or I'm soaking up the emotion of the performers. The entry points can vary every time and, when there is no agenda other than keeping an open mind, the experience can be allowed to flow naturally and organically.

The world we live in is our orchestra and each of us is an instrument within this global orchestra. Sometimes we are solo, sometimes we are part of a section, sometimes counting many bars' rest and observing the rest of the orchestra. We are all part of this orchestra and indeed we are the composers of the remarkable piece of life that lasts forever. Music is our everyday language and I don't believe there is such a thing as being unmusical. Music can happen anytime, anywhere, by anyone. It is the key to knowing ourselves, knowing the mechanics of the human brain and investing in the future of humankind.

To play an instrument is but one small aspect—albeit an important one—of what music really is. Each moment presents a kaleidoscope of tempo, rhythm, pitch, texture, dynamics which connect every living soul. Perhaps this is why I'm keen to say that music is our everyday medicine.

Just as food, water, shelter, and sleep are, music is completely accessible to each and every one of us, but how we choose to relate to it is something that only we ourselves can control. This brings the question of emotion and how music is a trigger to ignite emotions *between us* perhaps more than *within us*. Music forms a response to social interaction and can differ dramatically across societies and cultures.

The collection of narratives that compose *Missing Music* is both a celebration of the extraordinary music and musicians that are all around us, seen by some, unseen by many; heard by some, unheard by more. Yet this compact book also highlights the crisis of representation in mass media for far too many populations and regions. We live in a world where we constantly want to feel comfortable—within seconds—and not have to work at creating a journey of discovery. We can probably all think of occasions when someone from another culture has responded unusually to us and vice versa or when another's behavior has been misunderstood. We are driven to live in a culture where compliments are immediate to the point that they become overfamiliar. More than ever, we have the means to do our own digging into musical cultures and not be bound by perceived limitations of what the media sets. After all, what has been the most influential "performances" of our lives—the nursery rhymes sung by our parents? Seeing a school orchestra play? Seeing someone tap a nifty rhythm from a biscuit tin? Listening is about validating what makes each of us extraordinary. Richness is all around us in all forms and degrees. *Missing Music* invites us to extend the ways that we discover, interact with, and listen to the extraordinarily musical world we live in.

After all, the world is sound.

Dame Evelyn Glennie
Cambridgeshire, UK

INTRODUCTION

by the photographer
Marilena Umuhoza Delli

I was born in Italy to an Italian father and a Rwandan mother, but it took thirty years before I had a chance to listen to music in Kinyarwanda. I'd been raised instead with cassettes sung in French—the language of the Belgian colonizers. Therefore, it was a revelation to meet for the first time the Good Ones folk trio from the Rwandan countryside in the summer of 2009 when Ian was recording *Kigali Y'Izahabu* (Kigali of gold), the first of the forty-plus international records Ian and I have worked on since.

It was the very first album of original songs in Kinyarwanda to be widely distributed internationally. Multinationals and celebrities monopolize the market and silence the rest of the world—particularly the parts of the world that Western powers exploited as colonies and have since recolonized today. This is evidenced by radio stations in Kigali—and much of the rest of the globe—continuing to spit English-language music mostly from the US or Europe, silencing artists from rural and less-advantaged areas.

If it is true that words shape reality, privileged areas of the world dominating music tell us loads about their cultural and economic colonization, a colonization that denies the existence of most of the more than seven thousand languages spoken on our planet.

The power of *Missing Music* consists in recovering buried pieces of music from underrepresented areas of our earth, narrating stories like those from the ultracentenarian community living near the borders of Iran, or from the Botswana's desert plains, where shamans sing in Taa—a language now spoken by fewer than 2,500 people.

Working with Ian means not only meeting an artist and recording their music but also helping give voice to their story, providing an international stage where they can be listened to and valued. It means decolonizing a system that negates racialized people—particularly the poorest ones—who do not have the resources to publicize their music in *Billboard* on Grammys eve.

Intersectionality is at the core of Ian's work, because he aims to give voice to all identities, putting first poor/racialized/elderly/female/disabled artists. Full inclusion does not arise from skin color. Instead, racism was born and continues being fed by corporate bodies that, by tokenizing the racialized community, instrumentalize them and recolonize the world.

Inclusion also arises from language, a key element to understand the discrimination practiced by organizations who claim to celebrate global voices, when in fact they strangle the least advantaged and endangered ones. Working with Ian means treasuring the marginalized, often recording endangered languages such as Kikerewe in Tanzania, Gola in São Tomé, Talysh in Azerbaijan, and Saramaccan in Suriname.

A true ally, recently at a major international music conference we attended Ian calmly confronted a panel of experts for having only white people, who were over the age of fifty, and just one woman speaking about an art form born from African American culture. The packed room fell silent and all eyes turned when he spoke these truths, but after a few seconds of indignant suspense, they were forced to concede that he was right.

Ian's background, growing up with a disabled sister and having worked in locked psychiatric facilities in his teens and straight through his thirties, has afforded him a singular ability to connect with diverse individuals in a nonthreatening way and support them in their art. A musician since age five, for him this is not a hobby but a life.

It's been an honor working with Ian for all these years and a privilege filming and photographing such extremely talented musicians, individuals who have helped us grow both as artists and human beings.

PROLOGUE

There is no way
I can drive this coast
without thinking of your ghost.
It haunted me long before
you were ever gone.

This is a little book. But not about little people.

I hope to be forgotten. And the voices of the artists we've worked with, remembered. That is my prayer.

The miracle of a microphone is allowing the quietest singers to be heard—the living people already cut out of history.

These are timeless voices. Rather than seeking charity, theirs is the charitable act—truth offered without expecting anything in return. The only desire, connection.

We are interested in the places where countries dead-end, where the overlooked and minoritized live.

In contrast to cancelling people, we aim to laud and ratify those who have far too long been made invisible. To *un*-cancel them—the more than seven thousand languages speaking simultaneously, but silenced.

Chillingly, as corporations centralize escalating control of content across the globe, we are left a culture haunted by voices unheard.

Muffled and Muzzled

Most dreams live only in silence,
weakening over time.
But it's your memory
that keeps me here.
The most beautiful side of the mountain is
whichever you are on.

My parents were not music people. They existed in a murky zone—a few years too early for the birth of rock and roll, and already settled with their first child before the Beatles struck. Raised on Latin Mass, they were on the wrong side of the generation gap when pop culture cracked. Trying to be "cool" never even occurred to them. They were too preoccupied just trying to survive.

The closest my dad ever came to being a record buyer was diluted jazz—Dave Brubeck as an angst-less, deracinated stand-in for the form's rich history—or the Kingston Trio's frat-boy, WASPy folk.

Nonetheless, though my father wasn't a fan, he cried the day Michael Jackson died. He'd watched the King of Pop grow up, an eleven-year-old galvanizing television screens nationwide, and he too had been abused as a child. And because Michael mattered to us when we were children near the same age, he mattered to my dad. The distance in age was small enough that it was not a challenge for my father to imagine having lost one of his own.

Once when I was small, my dad clenched his eyes, leaned back, raised his face heavenward, and seemed on the verge of song—the point at which you either cry or sing. But the moment passed, and he left this world without our ever knowing his voice freed from words.

He held on to the pain like an heirloom, handed down intentionally or not. The only other time he looked more alive was right before his demise, kindled by the knowledge that his last seconds neared.

My mother would sometimes hum a tune to herself that other mothers hummed all over the world as well as generations before them—a song so basic that no one need write it. Instead, its existence was inevitable. A stepwise melody uniting families, carrying them elsewhere for a brief reprieve.

This morning, Elton John's "Philadelphia Freedom" came over the radio. My mom once sang along to the song—faking her way through, mumbling the words—without knowing or caring who the singer was. She'd never been to Philadelphia. Probably couldn't even find it on a map. But she knew what freedom felt like and, more importantly, the experience of having it denied.

My mother was driving along a throughway, not a red light in sight, her eyes welling with tears and her multitrack mind afire. When I hear the tune now, it takes me back in time, connecting to that moment—her death decades in the distance—when, however faint, she still held hope, and desire lit her from inside.

Hendrix, Pelé, Bruce Lee, and Dr. J adorned my suburban bedroom walls. But that wasn't enough. It was mere admiration rather than insight.

No one in my family, no one I ever knew spoke another language, at least openly. Surrounded by towns and streets with mispronounced Spanish names, we were an imaginary monoculture—default white, in a falsely binary world—with a large chunk of my working-class peers actually having at least one parent who was Latine, Indigenous American, or Asian. A bullied fat kid faking illness to skip school, I discovered Elvis via B-movies on morning television reruns for housewives. It was an inauspicious start. But a path forward, still.

I had a neighbor in the city that was strictly an auditory presence. I'd never seen them and had no idea even of their gender, age, size, or hair color. Spanning years, I heard their daily progression—from tentatively drilling scales as a novice on the clarinet to full-on, circular-breathing, free-jazz works.

Then one night I awakened and the player's profile was framed in her skylight, just from the shoulder up. Her eyes were closed as she blew into the clarinet and swayed as if in a trance, her curls cascading down, concealing her face. It looked as if she were levitating. The sight was as uncomfortably intimate as accidentally walking in on someone naked or having sex.

But, to this day, I still don't know who she is and have never recognized her passing on the street below. She remains an auditory apparition, a phantom.

Not long after my daughter was born, I bought a battered, upright minipiano. Acting as a magnet, nearly every child that has ever visited immediately runs to play it and within seconds invariably develops coherent musical structures. The consistency of this behavior reinforces what I've always believed—that music is within us all.

Nearly every person enacts improvisation daily. Conversation is dependent on it. Sadly, our culture exorcises these creative impulses, drilling people *not* to be musical and instead to fear expression—to seek proxies and reach for beauty only outside themselves.

ROAD MAPS

Small peers through the walls of his home.

1

fra fra

The Quiet Death of a Funeral Singer

There is a sad irony in writing an obituary for a man who spent his adult life as a funeral singer.

For decades, Mbabila "Small" Batoh led his trio, fra fra, in providing funeral music throughout rural northern Ghana.

"Small," as he was widely known, played a homemade kologo (two-stringed lute)—with dog tags attached to the end for rattles. He belted original songs like "You Can't Escape Death" and "No One Is an Orphan" with a tenor of raspy virtuosity.

He could riff almost endlessly and his performances grew freer and stronger past the ten-minute mark. At funerals, Small and his group would often play and sing from midday prior to long past dawn, ending only when the family felt that their loved one had been successfully sung onward from this world and into the afterlife.

But their music was rarely sorrowful. The group's exultant singing and dancing bear more than a passing resemblance to the boisterousness of New Orleans jazz funeral parades.

In February 2022, Batoh died, reportedly of COVID.

His death came during a career surge.

Following the 2020 release of fra fra's debut album, *Funeral Songs*, Batoh was invited to perform at Peter

Gabriel's annual WOMAD Festival in the England. It would have been the fulfillment of his long-held dream to travel outside of Ghana for the first time and perform abroad. The festival was twice postponed due to the pandemic but was scheduled to finally happen in July 2022, and Batoh remained eager to go.

I first encountered Small's music while visiting Ghana to record at the region's witch camps in late 2018. I heard tell of his funeral songs and searched him out. He expressed interest in making a record.

I set up and awaited the group at the assigned time and place—a gravel plot set amid former farmland slated for development near Small's home. More than an hour passed, and I began to fear that the trio wouldn't show.

Then in the distance I heard faint music. Small and his comrades were playing before coming into sight. The band arrived in procession, unhurriedly gyrating and zigzagging their way toward me and continuing without pause when they arrived.

It was there on the outskirts of Ghana's northern hub, Tamale, that beneath the midday sun I experienced one of the most powerful musical performances of a lifetime—the men encircling me and kicking up dust as they sang and danced.

Small was relatively short—standing approximately five feet four—and that's how he got his nickname. The name also referred to the "small" money people donated for serenades. Small actually came to prefer this one-name moniker—an act of reclamation from its derogatory connotations.

But none of the musicians had birth certificates, nor had they ever traveled outside of Ghana. Consequently, a lengthy bureaucratic process was undertaken—involving village chiefs attesting to the band members' identities and birthdates. After months of drudgery and tedium, passports for all three men had been successfully obtained.

I'd thought he was perhaps in his forties or early-fifties until I saw Small's official documents for his passport application. I was gobsmacked. Though he moved with the litheness of an adolescent—even duckwalking as he played—the man was a septuagenarian.

Small was born less than twenty-five miles from the Burkina Faso border, a two-day's drive and a world away from the modernity of the coastal capital, Accra. Like many from the north, Small never benefited from the postcolonial consolation prize of inherited English-language skills.

He sang in Frafra (also known as Farefare)—a language with only around three hundred thousand speakers spread across two nations and spoken by less than 2 percent of the citizens within Ghana. Similar to so many musicians from minoritized communities, he was singing in a foreign language even within his own nation.

Small, whose personal mantra was "be patient," proved among the too few rural musicians who overcome geographic, linguistic, and economic barriers to earn the right to play before a global audience.

This is not the first eulogy I've had to write for a sublime musician from a remote region. But given the many elder artists we work with and the massive global disparity in life expectancies, I fear it won't be my last. Each time serves as a reminder of my own advantage and the dreadful inequality on this earth. It weights my every breath.

Small devoted himself to alleviating the grief of others. His own voice replayed now helps those closest to him mourn. Yet, in a gut-wrenching twist, Small's family found themselves unable to fund his funeral. Quite prophetically, his final release was the single "Death Can Come at Any Time," from which all proceeds benefited his survivors and made possible his successful return to his home village skirting the northern border of Ghana.

For a lifetime Small led the way.

In the face of mortality, he danced.

2

Sister, Keeper

Cut My Soul in Two and There Would Still Be You

Growing up with a developmentally disabled older sister, I never knew a world without wheelchairs, primal noises, and slobber. Some of my earliest memories are of "spaghetti feed" benefits at her segregated school—the dining room a mass of tomato sauce, half-chewed meatballs, and drool. Acceptance of diverse ways of moving, articulating, and being were a nonnegotiable necessity.

This was back in the years when deinstitutionalization was brand spanking new and seeing a disabled person in the community still a novelty. Mainstreaming was not yet spoken of outside of liberal think tanks. Thus, our entire family was "mongoloid" by association, othered by default.

The truest test of character is how one treats those over whom we hold greater power. Anyone with a disabled sibling has likely experienced that weight of the inequality between family members, the guilt carried for the abuses of power that occur, however unintentionally. They've known the desolation of being mocked and ostracized, while simultaneously comprehending that their experience is secondhand and infinitesimal compared to their family member's, and that the person you love as much as anyone in the world is forced from birth to shoulder the weight of that exclusion alone.

Living with a sister who is intellectually impeded but spiritually superior is a sobering affair. Jane's attention is

My sister Jane and her colleagues record
at their East Bay workshop.

on what's being conveyed more than explicitly said—the inflection, subtle changes in the brow or voice, and utmost, the sincerity or lack thereof.

Our mother was a psychiatric nurse who was also intermittently a psychiatric patient, a not-so-uncommon combination. Often Jane, our older brother, and I were left to parent each other as best we could.

Though I was technically self-taught on guitar, my sister schooled me more about music and dance than I—or anyone else—ever could. She provided a daily demonstration of freedom, simplicity, and directness in expression.

She was my conservatory, my mentor. Modeling resourcefulness—to work with whatever little you've got for maximum effect.

Sadly, my sister is now bedridden. The same person who danced with the abandon of Cab Calloway is now motionless—as is Mr. Calloway, as eventually we all will be.

When I went to see my sister last in California, she was nearly comatose—unable to lift her limbs and seemingly not recognizing my brother and me. So the staff tried to quickly usher us out the door, but I hadn't come that far just to leave her in such a state.

So, I decided to try behaving exactly like the little brother I was. I picked up a pillow and started hitting her lightly in the face with it—a good old-fashioned pillow fight. Jane came alive—and quite appropriately grew a bit pissed off.

Earlier in the year, I'd sent her a CD player and a batch of CDs, but they seemed to have gone mostly unused. So I plugged in the player and started putting on music from our childhood.

First it was Tony Orlando & Dawn, whom she'd always loved. Orlando also had a sister with Down syndrome and my sister, Jane, adored him in the 1970s when his weekly prime-time program ran on television. I later read that he'd learned to sing and communicate while trying to relate to his sister, who was nonverbal. This seemed connected to why my sister responded to him so strongly.

As the CDs spun, I started singing and dancing, and ever so faintly my sister began moving her left pinkie. Next, she started singing nonverbally, mostly muttering. The staff that worked there were shocked and overjoyed—pulling out their phones and filming. Then we put on the Village People, and Jane started also moving her opposing hand. She sang louder and louder before breaking into laughter and clapping. Then we let loose Springsteen, and in full-on clown mode I belted "The River" and "Born to Run" to her.

And if you put a Michael Jackson song on, the motor skills of everyone in the room improve instantly.

Jane gleams a smile during more carefree, pre-COVID times.

Jane became fully animated and was returned to us for an hour. Almost sixty, she neared the life expectancy of those with Down syndrome from her generation. I knew that this quite likely could be the last time I'd ever see her.

Just moments before, it had seemed like she would never be that present again. Instead, there was a resurrection. The music had done that, sparking something deep within her. For the length of those tunes, she rose.

All the physical therapists, doctors, and psychotropic medications couldn't do what a few shitty pop tunes effortlessly achieved. Neurologists have discovered that music activates more parts of the brain simultaneously than any other stimulus. Here stood proof.

As an infant, Jane had been born more than two months premature and then dropped even more weight. After being incubated for weeks, the doctors ultimately sent her "home to die." That she instead endured for decades is a testament to the strength of her spirit.

Due to Jane's sudden behavioral changes and physical decompensation, we suspected what unknown horrors had been visited upon her in a residential home during the first months of COVID lockdown. The panic attacks that followed substantiated our fears. Thankfully those alarming episodes have slowly receded. As she has done throughout her days, Jane hung on, defying the odds. Though her ability to ambulate, feed herself, speak, and remain continent have vanished, her tenacity has not been without purpose.

She was fighting her way back to a semblance of her former emotional peace.

Through it all, her light remains.

The 101-year-old former shepherd Isakhan reminisced of his mother and thanked us for "bringing me back to the sky."

3

The Oldest Voice in the World (Azerbaijan)

Thank You for Bringing Me Back to the Sky

My life is good.
It is like a flower.
My life is as long as a tree,
like a stone in the river.

In Azerbaijan, I was cautioned not to use my first name because it sounded Armenian.

Military memorials stood at nearly every intersection and exit, and the border war ominously broke out again hours after we arrived. Wars tend to not truly end completely, but to take on different forms, resonating through interpersonal aftershocks. Here guns must be rented for hunting season. Firearm licenses are allegedly harder to come by than master's degrees. A country that's recently known or continues to know war grasps the nonnecessity of guns in daily life.

In the capital, Baku, oil platforms clung to the Caspian Sea like ticks and a ghost city skirted the coastline, skyscraper skeletons sitting unfinished for over a decade. On the street below our hotel room, a jackhammer acquired B.B. King's soul, wailing out high-on-the-neck, bent notes every time the machine was pivoted.

Well-off Muslim tourists descend from nearby nations because here they can purchase and openly drink wine and spirits without scrutiny, but still get halal meat easily.

Shahbaji, 101, said the secret to life was that she was loved.

In the southern mountains of the country—just miles from the Iran border—are the villages of the "long-livers." Legend has it that the world's oldest man hailed from there—having survived to age 168 and fathered his twenty-third child when he was a mere 136, spanning two of my father's lifetimes in one.

We ventured there as a deliberate rejection of ageism, a counter to mass media's fetishizing youth. I've often preferred singers' voices as they age—Little Jimmy Scott, Billie Holliday, Sinatra, Merle Haggard. Less pristine, but gaining depth and nuance. They are the exception, though. Most stars fall into caricature over time. It's hard to remain a truthful singer when you're a millionaire and overly adored.

At the other end of the spectrum, children's voices routinely teem with honesty. Not the six-year-old pros who try to belt like Aretha Franklin or Mariah Carey, but six-year-olds who reflect their own stage of life and its distinct complexities.

More than blatantly bad art, the ultimate cultural crime is mediocrity. Failure is far more exciting than banality. It's the netherworld between the extremes that is the most asphyxiating. Unfortunately, that is where the bulk of commercial music resides.

We visited village after rural village ravaged by COVID. The tale was sadly the same, most residents over a hundred had died in recent months. That included the oldest known woman in the country. Years prior, the news of her being officially named as the nation's oldest person had been widespread, but her death remained conspicuously unreported for over a year.

As with every project, there is a phantom voice thwarted, the "one that got away," left to exist only in our imagination.

There were stringed instruments on the currency but nowhere else found. We passed valley floors tilted as if sifting gold, and not a single tourist item was sighted for sale anywhere.

Our driver with the "Sweet Home Alabama" ringtone was labeled a foreigner by the minority Talysh speakers. He had learned to speak English by listening to Zeppelin and Ozzy. The search for elders and some of the rawest voices in the world was juxtaposed by the driver's soundtrack of over-the-top production—Def Leppard, REO Speedwagon, Backstreet Boys, Boston, Meat Loaf, Journey, Bon Jovi, Whitesnake.

There were more cows than cars on the road—the part of the nation that capitalist campaigners don't want you to see, a sharp contrast to the neon-lit, futuristic skyline of the capital city.

"The government is rich, but the people are poor," locals testified.

Elders lined blocks predawn, sweeping dirt sidewalks with branch brooms. Like everywhere, people were up early trying to put some order to their world.

We got stuck in the mud, a worse obstacle than ice and snow, and were only pulled to safety by some castoff USSR military truck that emerged miraculously from the zero-visibility fog. Passing a hundred feet of downward sloping, unpaved road had become a slow-motion crisis—as uncrossable as a canyon. The main village's name in fact translates to "mud."

The elephantine 4×4 SUV had proven unfit. Instead, a gutted two-door compact with oversized tires was the only means other than on foot or donkey that villages could be reached.

So we ended up in need of a guide for our guide.

The seatbelt-less, local driver texted while steering with one knee and skirting a snowy cliff. Our urbane companion screeched in fright, as we faced the irony of dying prematurely a few football fields short of the village where the oldest person in history had lived. The razor-edged mountains there were enough to raise Ansel Adams from the dead, sparked by an urge to destroy his own aggrandized negatives.

To our Azerbaijani-speaking friend from the city, the locals' words were completely unintelligible. Even the Talysh speaker from the valley below could only make out less than 80 percent of what was being said in the remote mountain villages. And so they enacted how languages

Sargiz, 103, sang to herself while alone and related that the key to long life was to "eat lots of butter."

disappear—bridge words from the dominant, national language began to entwine and eventually overtake.

Ultimately, we discovered person after person—lying on floor-bound mattresses as if awaiting our arrival.

Theirs were voices featuring distortion boxes built by time. While recording, I removed my headphones more than once thinking there was some malfunction in the machinery only to realize that what I was hearing was the singer's pure tone. This was a rare instance of many people not making the cut for being too young—a mere ninety or eighty-six failed to impress. These are lives lived in analog, standing as an antidote to artificial intelligence art and Auto-Tuned vocals.

Other countries like Japan and Guadeloupe are also recognized for having a high preponderance of centenarians. Currently, the oldest known person in the world is 116-year-old San Francisco–born Spaniard, María Branyas Morera, who sagely advises to "stay away from toxic people." Before passing in 2020, the world's oldest man was 116-year-old South African Fredie Blom, who staggeringly remained a daily cigarette smoker for his entire life (and died just after quitting).

In the Talysh Mountains there is much debate about the reasons for the longevity found there. Some say it's the daily physical exertion, clean air, and spring water; others point to the use of rare mountain herbs. But by far the most consistent life advice the village elders offered spat in the face of every New Age prescription known: "Eat lots of butter."

One man sang for us but said he could no longer bring himself to play the flute since his grandson had died.

A 101-year-old woman we met, Shahbaji, had given birth to fourteen children over her lifetime. She lamented the recent loss of a grandson in the border battle with Armenia that she labeled a "rich man's war." Seated, she repeatedly pounded the table before her so hard that the teacups rattled in their saucers, spiking the LED meters.

She scolded, "Drinking tea without lemon is like a wedding night without consummation."

Amid a household in preparation for a wedding party, another 103-year-old woman's son kept interrupting and instructing his mother how to sing. Afterward she sang worse—with more pep, but less honestly.

On occasions like this album, where singers have requested anonymity, it is baffling how reflexively misguided politically correct actors have viewed it as suspicious rather than exhibiting sensitivity to the multitude of reasons why someone of advanced age might desire privacy.

Each person's living environment was used for instrumentation—the wood-burning furnace providing heat for the house, a walker, their own footsteps, a broken bedroom door, the farm's flour mill.

What was maybe the most striking thing of all was how often many of the centenarian singers sang of their mothers.

One man, Isakhan, asserted that "the shepherd sees everything."

Midsong, that shepherd was overcome and stood to leave the room after having crooned a song his mother had sung. In awkward suspense, we feared our visit had caused him unnecessary upset or injury. But when he returned, he beamed, grabbed my hand, and kissed it repeatedly.

"Thank you for bringing me back to the sky," he said.

Mandolin is the featured
instrument in Rohingya music.

4

Rohingya Refugees

Once I Had a Home

The security guard at the connecting airport in Dubai laughed when he saw our boarding passes for Dhaka. At first he wouldn't explain this reaction and just kept smiling.

Finally, he uttered, "You're really going to *my* country. And with your family? I've never seen anyone going there."

With little choice otherwise, we took it as a good omen.

He said he was from Chittagong, a place reportedly so dangerous that the Bangladesh government requires foreigners to provide a minimum of ten days' notice before attempting to enter. And that was exactly where we were headed.

But considering that the United States has the highest rate of gun violence and incarceration in the world, it's hard to keep an entirely straight face when Americans warn of violence elsewhere on the planet.

To be the only white person on a packed plane is to experience for a scant few hours the degree of difference that far too many endure over a lifetime. For a vegetarian to arrive during a holiday when cows and mutton are slaughtered in the streets is a tad ironic. The festivity's goal is sharing—to ensure "every Muslim has meat." Livestock loitered and sat in the road, seemingly in protest, a desire to die on their own terms.

Burkas dotted the longest uninterrupted beach in the world, Cox's Bazar, reaching almost a hundred miles in length. Nearby stood the real Long Beach Hotel, at least to those in this neck of the woods. Rather than local music, Kenny G looped in every elevator we rode in—he, a true elevator muzak master.

Hardly a "small" country, Bangladesh has the eighth-largest population in the world and is one of the most densely populated. It's estimated that as many as three million people died during their battle for independence from Pakistan in 1971. Known for its humidity, the nation has never recorded a temperature below freezing.

There was a windowless breastfeeding box at the airport to provide modesty, and sleeping rent-a-cops at checkpoints. We repeatedly passed signs advertising the Tourist Police. Their official motto: "We Care Tourist."

Due to the standard of living in the north being worlds apart and the language spoken a different one, a man from the capital assured, "Don't worry, they consider me a foreigner down south here, too."

In 1982, the Rohingya people were made stateless on the land they've lived on for thousands of years and became *un*listed as one of the Myanmar government's 135 "national races." Today, the Myanmar military rulers forbid the use of the term Rohingya, instead referring to the Rohingya as "illegal immigrants." The Myanmar military aggressions have been declared an official genocide, and experts state that the Rohingya are one of the most persecuted minorities in the world.

Now, Russian speed is flooding into the region across the same Myanmar border area that the Rohingya people were forced across—warfare waged in another form.

A few years back a billionaire tech titan visited Myanmar for a spiritual retreat. When criticized for not observing the international boycott of the nation, he was unrepentant, avowing that he planned to possibly return again. His is a case study in why such acute concentrations of power and plentitude are antithetical to democracy.

The Rohingya refugee camp is estimated as the largest in the world and currently houses almost a million people. Most residents are not allowed to exit the camp, so we came to them. Gangs operate within the camp, and women are often exploited for sex work due to food shortages. Currently, families are provided eight cents a day for meals, yet a single egg costs eleven cents.

With 96 percent humidity filling the summer air, the sweat soaked my body in seconds, pouring off my face and onto the equipment, presenting a new operational hazard for the recording deck.

Here I achieved the dubious distinction of contracting food poisoning on a fifth continent. I stood dehydrated in the midday sun as calls to prayer were sounded from all sides. People bowed down to pray as I fell on all fours and blew chunks across an unfinished rooftop. If ever there was an opportunity for religious conversion or a sign from God, it was now.

It's highly unlikely, though, that a terrorist's improvised explosive device will be what gets you. Rather, it'll be traces of E. coli, which make for an effective crash diet to rid of some of the last, few stubborn pounds, but not one that's recommendable. Somehow I muddled through and completed the day's recording, dazed.

I believe that you should fear no one and everyone at the same time. But if there is one tell for danger, it's ego. Narcissists are the most likely to make a mountain out of a molehill and fight over any perceived threat to their inflated sense of self. Instead, unless presented with overwhelmingly evidence otherwise, we must actively choose to believe in each individual's goodness, for even gangsters have heart— no matter how selective, no matter how small.

Mohammad Rashid sings with a weariness that tells of the horrors he's witnessed.

One recording spot was down a muddy cul-de-sac. If the all-ages mob trailing us—both hostile and gleeful— was any indication, nonlocals had rarely visited. The house itself could only be reached by toeing the balance beam of a cement basin for twenty yards that contained the knee-deep, stagnant sewage from the community. This was the dark side of the coastal area, life in the shadow of oceanfront tourist hotels and the constant chorus of dueling rickshaw horns piercing the air.

We did not prompt the singers what they should write about. Without fail, though, group after group sang about only two topics—the impact of the genocide *and* love songs.

Titles like "We Were Forced across the River (My Mother Died from the Pain)" and "The Army Tortured Us and Raped My 12-Year-Old Cousin Before Killing Her" repeatedly and consistently revealed the atrocities.

Though many female singers were invited to participate, none did so due to local religious customs that frown upon (and in some cases even ban) women singing solo publicly.

For the male groups, the mandolin was the core instrument, and they used a mop bucket drum and tree twigs for mallets. Like so many people we've worked with, they all chose to sing while sitting cross-legged on the floor or dirt—literally grounding themselves.

As so often is the case, one of the strongest singers emerged spur-of-the-moment—a twelve-year-old who looked half his age but sang "If You Love Me, I Will Build You a Small Home (I Will Give Anything for You)" with a throaty, weary tone.

On so many projects there are musicians or styles presented that would likely have broad appeal to "world music" aficionados and beyond. But these are the exactly the elements that are of little interest to us. We're instead invested in noncommercial music—an active opposition against standardization's oppression—and instead pine for

Over eight hundred thousand people live stateless and
suspended in the largest refugee camp in the world,
where families are currently provided eight cents a day
for food (while a single egg costs eleven cents).

heartfelt sounds we've never heard before versus journey-
men retreads.

Field recording is not about just pointing a microphone
at someone and hitting record. It requires bringing a lifetime of listening and close study of idiosyncratic musical
moments that transcend time, borders, and genre.

Random social media representation police have
become so draconian that recently they've begun sending
unsolicited emails demanding to know if rural artists' music
was mixed with any effects or edited in any way. But the

music they're inquiring about is typically solo, a cappella singing, which is the purest musical representation of any individual—literally *their* voice unadulterated. The first and last thing a person does on this earth is make a sound—starting with a scream and ending with a rattle. And I present each voice with the least possible adjustment—virtually unmediated from the singer's throat to the listener's ear.

But that is not enough to assuage many self-appointed guardians of strangers, none of whom would ever demand to know what signal processing was used on Justin Bieber's or a K-pop group's voices, information that could not be provided even if attempted. The sheer amount of manipulation of the source would require algebraic formulas to explain. Some artists not only were heavily Auto-Tuned but also had their vocals punched in and overdubbed line by line, word by word, and even syllable by syllable.

The people we've worked with on the margins are not concerned about appropriation, but rather misappropriation—the removal of allocation—which they live daily.

Most people in Bangladesh reportedly prefer Indian singers to local ones. The taxi driver had loads of Bollywood music in his library but not a single song from Bangladesh.

As one vocalist described the ordeal he'd faced being exiled from his land, his voice suddenly broke and he began quivering. Soon the emotion radiated to his bandmates and then others assembled. It's rare to see a group of grown men weeping openly together, especially those who were otherwise so stoic. I was overcome, but refrained, turning away.

Their pain was not mine to claim.

The Gue Pa collective perform a circle dance under the rain.

5

N'golá (São Tomé)

Our Ancestors Swam to Shore

São Tomé and Príncipe, a two-island Central African nation, is one of only thirteen countries that lie *on* the equator. Their motto is "léve, léve," which translates to "slow, slow."

The villages feature buildings designed by time, textured by daily waves of rainstorms. Shop signs in metal now speak in absence of their intended message, placards rusting away blankly in the sun. Ranging free in the streets, pigs command the land rather than goats—evidence that it's a Christian nation, not an Islamic one. At all corners, clothesline choreography pays witness to the wind, and anyone who doubts that African regional cuisines are among the most vibrant in the world has never tried baobab tree ice cream.

On the southern coast of São Tomé live the ances-tors of escaped slaves from Angola. They reportedly swam ashore after a shipwreck on Seven Stone Island, visible just off the east coast. Most descendants work fishing the coast and speak Angolar Creole—also called "N'Golá" by its native speakers. The language heavily features Kimbundu, a Bantu language from inland Angola, where many had been enslaved.

In São Tomé, "gola" historically has been used as a slur designating dumb or "retarded." The ruling aristocracy regards the N'golá people as the lowest class—as if they are

Far from the tourists, where the road runs out at the
southern end of São Tomé Island, music lives.

still being punished for having escaped, for having been
captured as slaves.

The local traveling with us from the city couldn't understand but stray words of the language. There are fewer than
seven thousand speakers remaining, and they represent not
even 3 percent of the entire country's population of only
around two hundred thousand.

Often, language develops as much as a way to *not* be understood—speaking faster, altering accents, slurring or swallowing syllables—so that outsiders are left in the dark.

It's hard to fully fathom the generational trauma of having been minoritized within one's own land so viciously that one is captured and forcibly emigrated, only to escape due to a tragedy at sea, and then being reenslaved when the Portuguese settlers "discovered" their well-established community by accident.

The "African Music" channel broadcast mostly Brazilian artists. The Portuguese connection continues robustly, with the island somewhat isolated from the African continent, yet benefitting strongly from Portuguese-language tourists. A local musician told me he had no idea who Burna Boy, Ladysmith Blacksmith Mambazo, Angelique Kidjo, or even Fela was.

Past the chocolate plantation where the paved road peters out, an elder led us to his village. Still in knee-high, rubber work boots and coveralls, he cobbled together a crew ad hoc and launched into songs beside a cove where young children bathed and dove for octopus. Clearly, there was "no lifeguard on duty" in the entire nation.

During the recordings, the kids were better behaved than the drunks who'd congregated—wasted on palm wine and spirits. Nearby, one girl roller-skated across gravel and with only one skate. But she thoughtfully stopped to wait each time a new song began.

One group played a gue pa, an instrument meant to resemble a canoe that the leader straddled and played with a Phillips-head screwdriver as his bandmates circled and sang.

When recording, I'm not there to teach people anything. I am there to learn. I always try to position myself lower physically than the people I'm working with. My duty is to listen, not to judge or control.

I take it as a given that the more one tries to control another, influence is actually lost. The acted upon individual withdraws their autonomous and intrinsic cooperation.

No matter how positive the intentions, in situations of great inequity we risk compounding the inequality rather than remedying it. Thus, we must work resolutely to bridge the gap rather than exacerbate it.

More than once I've worked with mixing engineers that treat roots music as beneath them—measuring value in terms of the number of tracks, revering cerebral, math-like elaborations more than truth. Their bias masks deeper prejudices.

We visited a regional rock star's mansion, sporting so much glass it resembled a rest-stop restaurant. It sat around the corner from where sewage ran in the streets between huts, and I had to straddle streams of shit as we recorded. And like everywhere in the world, that rock star kept us waiting for over an hour, ultimately never to show.

Describing one of that star's songs, a man in his twenties said, "It a very old song."

When pressed as to precisely how old, he replied, "I don't know. Liiiike . . . 1992?" That was exactly the era—*my* era—that I feared he'd define as vintage.

In the fishing village where the main road fades before vanishing entirely, we waited for some musicians to arrive.

An open-air bar adorned its walls with pages torn from porn mags, like an artless *Kama Sutra*. The streets were stuffed with people smoking and an eruption of shirts-off fisticuffs between two young warriors without a war. The clash was broken up only when an elder leaned on a truck horn, which bleated hoarsely from decades of overuse.

Every corner we ventured, the report was the same: No one in town had a "viola" (guitar). The one guitar we finally located was orphaned without a player. It was an instrument tuned by chance.

The Pires family was met along the roadside after
some formal singers nearby failed to deliver.

Unexpectedly, when we returned a ten-year-old boy
had built his own in two days' time—three strings made
from fishing line nailed and tied to a piece of plywood with
a crushed aluminum can for a resonator. He played with a
fervor unfound by weekend warriors noodling on limited-
edition Les Pauls and Strats at warehouse music stores
throughout the world.

6

Parchman Prison Prayer

Some Mississippi
Sunday Morning

Instead of attending the Grammys, I opted to fly to Mississippi and record with prisoners at the notorious Parchman Prison. I had faith that the "amateur" voices there would be more compelling. The institution has a substantial musical history, with Son House, Bukka White, and even Elvis Presley's father, Vernon Presley, as former residents. The Black Panther Party's Stokely Carmichael and other civil rights Freedom Riders were also jailed here.

With just over a week's notice I'd taken a red-eye flight and would only be allowed a few hours inside the walls to record. One wrong turn detour on the way from the airport or a single delayed flight and the whole enterprise would've been moot.

As I snaked along two-lane byways, I passed raised tin huts edging swampland. Road signs frequently reminded that bridges ice before roads, a recurring metaphor of sorts.

A friend had warned that the prison is a place few people visit. In reality, it is a place far too many go. With over two million people incarcerated, the United States currently leads the world in both the total number of people in prison and the incarceration rate. And Mississippi has the second-highest incarceration rate in the country at more than six times that of the state with the lowest (Vermont).

The bucolic setting of the prison belies the reality found inside.

Mississippi is also the state with the highest percentage of African American citizens and is the poorest in the nation. The tired rationalization "boys will be boys," would be better translated to "*white* boys will be white boys," since they're systematically granted greater forgiveness and benefit of the doubt. African Americans are unconscionably imprisoned at five times or more the rate of whites according to the NAACP and other sources.

Mississippi's oldest penitentiary, Parchman was established in 1901, just a hop and a skip to the northwest of Money, Mississippi, where Emmett Till was later heinously murdered. It has one of the highest rates of prisoner mortality in the nation and experiences ongoing riots.

Also just around the bend is the Delta Blues Museum in Clarksdale, near where John Lee Hooker and B.B. King were raised, Sam Cooke and Ike Turner born, Bessie Smith died, and legend contends Robert Johnson sold his soul to the Devil at the crossroads (a meeting point where two major Indigenous American routes had intersected).

Composed of "farms," the prison occupies twenty-eight square miles and houses the death row for both men and women in Mississippi. Such is the penitentiary's history and size that they even have their own cemeteries. Only this century did they end the practice of "forced field labor," the successor to chain gangs picking cotton before sunup. An aging British blues fan told me he'd visited Parchman in the 1980s and was given an impromptu tour on what happened to be that guard's last day. The retiring officer confessed his one career regret was having never had an opportunity to personally execute anyone.

Scandals rocked the prison in recent years, with multiple deaths and homicides. This led Jay-Z to file a class-action suit on behalf of the inmates due to the "barbaric" and "abhorrent" conditions with rat infestations and raw sewage filling common areas.

After years of bureaucratic finagling to make my visit possible, the gate guard waved me through without even searching me or my gear. I could've easily been smuggling bazookas or kilos.

I parked, tossed together what little kit I'd been allowed, and within minutes of saying hello, we were recording.

But no matter how much time is allotted, I feel a similar urgency. The most invaluable and finite resource artistically is human energy. I learned decades ago while working in psychiatric emergency that anything you can do now, do it. It remains unknown what crises await. Second chances simply may not exist.

Due to restrictions on video and photos, the only artifact from this meeting are the sounds—making the voices all the more ethereal and ghostly. This stands in stark contrast to increasingly image based music. Rapists, murderers, and sex offenders vocalizing lifetimes of hurt.

Just as at Zomba Prison in Malawi, one man was imprisoned for having stabbed to death a rival musician, morbid proof that jealously and resentment are universal.

One inmate's voice was so deep, it sounded like the Mississippi River bed itself was singing, enough to make Barry White seem like a soprano.

Another was a seventy-three-year-old former rock 'n' roll singer who'd survived prison, become a chaplain, and found God.

His mantra: "You've to get out of prison while you're still in prison."

One man had his own name tattooed on his wrist, as if he might forget it, the way the outside world seemingly had—like institutionalized kids having their initials written in the collar, sole, or waistband of every item of clothing.

All had eyes leaden with regret, hooded to protect themselves from the too much they'd already seen. A veil of sadness seemed to shroud, an inescapable regret with which their environment confronted them relentlessly. Voices softened and textured by mistakes made rang as testament to the singers no longer being the people they were before.

Studies have shown that very few individuals repeat violent crimes past the age of forty-five. At midlife some natural tipping point seems to occur where the spirit

One inmate committed his faith to ink.

catches up from the body's having raced ahead under the hormonal surge of youth. That is one of the most pragmatic assessments against the death penalty—its lack of necessity, its sheer redundancy.

In Texas, an experiment was once done where some judges voluntarily experienced being incarcerated for a month. The results were graphic. The judges who participated sentenced people to prison less often, and when they did issue prison sentences, the lengths were dramatically shorter. Even a single hour or day takes on meaning when you've lived it bone deep, in real time.

How many people intermittently in our midst are toying with the edge, wavering toward an irreversible abyss. Almost none of us have not found ourselves drifting toward such chasms, only to be saved by chance, inertia or ambivalence. I do not believe in Original Sin but *inevitable* sin. All of us are imperfect to varying degrees.

Though many outstripped me in size and strength, not only were these men *not* menacing but they demonstrated greater pains than most to show their good intentions—that they had "learned their lesson."

Most songs were covers of gospel standards but delivered so imbued with subtext that they were transformed almost unrecognizably from the source material.

When an atheist takes to the music, genre and preconceptions have been transcended, and following the release of the album I witnessed this happening a hundred times over.

A triumph of this recording was its successful integration of the inmates, whose services are often held separately, in part due to racial tensions. Different clusters of prisoners didn't start out sitting together. Some even sat alone. But the boundaries gradually dissolved. It ended in hugs, laughter, high-fives, and every single person in the room standing and playing together uninterruptedly for ten minutes of unity.

These were voices unchained, if only for those few hours—expressing a depth of freedom otherwise denied and restrained.

7

Saramaccan Sound (Suriname)

Where the River Bends Is Only the Beginning

I cut down a tree.
I made two boats.
They will carry me to the sea.

Entering the rain forest—"the lungs of the earth"—we rode upriver to villages reached only by boat. We passed communities that had been swallowed whole, as well as many of the still-existing villages that may soon no longer be there—flooded by the dams and the rising tides. For now, though, naked children bathed and played on the banks, scenes probably largely unchanged from centuries past. The river remains the lifeline.

The closer a place is to America or Europe, the more likely it's been dominated by Western culture, as well as disproportionately documented. Mass media tends to rotely retrace colonialist pathways. Think Mali, Cuba, India, Nigeria, South Africa, and their somewhat arbitrary designations as mystically musical.

Liberation from the imperialistic pull only occurs wherever English (and to a lesser degree globally in the current era, French) stops being spoken and white faces become seldom seen.

Russian-made shotguns are standard issue for most river residents. Clearly disregarding or not well-versed in

Recording by the river, the only means to reach local villages.

firearms safety, one middle-aged man let his rifle hang casually off his shoulder and every time he turned, the huge barrel pointed directly toward a group of children standing immediately beside him.

"You never enter the jungle without taking a gun. If you see something to eat, you kill it. We don't have set meal times, as we sometimes don't have any food. So mealtime is whenever you have something available."

In the post-COVID global crisis, the price of cooking oil had skyrocketed. An elder reported repeated deaths of men so desperate that they were sneaking into mines to try to scavenge gold scraps. Just that past week, another young man lost his life trying.

The primary village we made camp in only has power from dusk to midnight, and that service only started two years ago. Since then, it has become a hub where people travel from neighboring villages to charge their cellphones.

The singers were Saramaccan. Linguists consider the Saramaccan language notable because its vocabulary is based on two European source languages, English (30 percent) and Portuguese (20 percent), and various West and Central African languages (50 percent), but it diverges considerably from all of them. The African component accounts for over half of the vocabulary, allegedly the highest percentage in the Americas. A language born from fugitive slaves, Saramaccan camouflages meaning by shuffling around accented syllables and inverting tones.

The less-highlighted history of Latin America is the other trans-Atlantic slave trade—the southerly trajectory—and the populations that helped make those societies but remain oppressed or denied.

"We come from one belly, all from the same mother..." was a theme intoned more than once.

An alarm bell was rung the first night we were there. A local informed us that this was an ominous notice that someone from the village had passed while away in the city.

And in the morning we awoke predawn to the universal rural soundtrack—roosters (with crickets and frogs providing the nighttime lullaby). A local waved from outside our window, a bit overzealously—not genuinely friendly, just still wasted from the night before.

Suriname has a little over half a million people and though it is physically the smallest nation in South America, it is one of the least densely populated places on earth.

One group took us to the river's edge to perform death rites that cannot be conducted in the village lest risking that some people might be taken by the spirit. The musicians broke twigs from a neighboring mangrove tree, then scratched them to wake the dead. The formal funeral process takes six weeks. Mourners only sing at the end, in celebration.

Robert Jabini displayed a seemingly inexhaustible
ability to compose new ballads on the spot.

A group of Rastas draped in white gowns beguiled with
beats and chants, the lead drummer busting polyrhythms
like an Art Blakey prototype. The fact that the Saramaccan
language includes a rarely found implosive sound no doubt
lends itself to such intricacies.

One eight-piece, electrified band rocked the thatch-roof hut. Though some of the best recordings in history have been made on the worst equipment, what sounds powerful live—loud amps, bashed drums—paradoxically often translates weakly into a swirl when recorded.

Acoustic guitars were the rule, though.

A brother duo commenced by playing a Chuck Berry song but reported that they did not know where the tune came from.

"It's just something we heard."

The reference to a "ding-a-ling" seemed lost in transmission, converted phonetically from risqué to mere jibber-jabber.

The main writer, singer, and mentor was Robert Jabini. A military man, he stood less than five feet six but with an imposing build. His gym, a lifetime of hard work. He plays the guitar upside-down due to being left-handed.

With his mournful melodies and handlebar mustache, it was as if Merle Haggard had been raised in the Amazon instead of Bakersfield.

This is the other "American" folk music, one that made a left turn before reaching the Gulf Coast.

And as is so often the case, the best songs emerged only *after* we were done recording. The equipment had to be set up three more times and lugged to the men on the front porch, as they sang almost nonstop through the night, growing freer as they drained the bottles of rum. They seemed in command of an almost inexhaustible ability to conjure new songs. Finally, they concluded with an anthem written on the spot: "One Mother, Two Hearts."

The recordings led to the Saramaccan Sound (Suriname) duo being invited to the UK for the WOMAD festival. This was the first opportunity ever for either of the men to travel outside Suriname.

Mr. Jabini received his visa, but his brother, Dwight Sampi, was denied. The government was splitting atoms—refusing one of two nearly identical applications that were submitted at the same time, on the same day. Jabini was left to go solo, absent his partner's harmonies and guitar counterpoint—Simon without Garfunkel, so to speak.

The official reason for the visa denial was the officer saw no reason for Sampi "to leave the UK" at the end of his visit. The more evident reality was Sampi had no reason *to* stay. He speaks no English, knows no one in the UK, has long held a job with the government, and has a wife and four children at home.

Far from an aspiring immigrant, while in England Dwight's brother Robert literally wrapped himself onstage in the Suriname flag, wearing it like a superhero cape. He found the local British food repulsive. His face expressed disgust at almost every option offered and he ate so little during his five-day stay that we feared he might suffer malnutrition.

He longed for home.

After a triumphant solo performance on the WOMAD stage—during which audience members stood steadfast and devout, weathering a rainstorm—Jabini returned to Paramaribo and was serenaded in the airport arrivals hall by a contingent of guitar-wielding members of the Saramaccan community dressed in traditional attire, headed by his brother Dwight.

Unbeknownst to us, Robert's uncle had left this world days before Robert's departure, and Robert was left to wrestle with his grief alone. Even more sadly, Robert was met upon his return with the devastating news that his own father had died suddenly during the singer's brief absence. This bitterly recalled the 2013 ordeal of Alfred from the Malawi Mouse Boys: after traveling out of his country for the first time ever, he returned mere days afterward to find that his young father had passed away.

Kenneth shares songs of villages lost to the floods.

I am most interested in the essence of what is being said versus word-for-word translation. If a singer tells me they are singing about birds or sadness, then what's being conveyed rather than explicitly stated takes precedent.

The physical place where a recording occurs is an accompanying instrument in any music made. In this case, my laptop and two mics succumbed to the humidity—an offering to the sound gods. Enveloped by forest and yards away from the river, the humidity seeping into the microphones is almost audible. And steel-string guitars are not an option. They rust almost instantly. So the mellower tone of nylon strings defines the land.

Hurriedly, retracing our steps back to the airport, we left—as so often has been the case in past experiences—without ever recording the originally intended artist. He'd canceled on us daily. And in the end, we vacated the country without our passports even being checked, waltzing through an unstaffed border.

8

Bhutan Balladeers

Your Face Is Like the Moon, Your Eyes Are Stars

"The young people are not interested in our folk music. The #1 band here is AC/DC, and then a bunch of other English-language artists."

Almost on cue, a teenager turned the corner in an AC/DC tee. Then a few blocks later, another. But those heshers stood out among the overwhelming majority of city dwellers who still donned traditional dress daily.

When the local was asked if there was anyone from Africa living in Bhutan, he replied, "Yes. Three."

I thought he meant countries, but he was citing individuals.

And when asked about America, he said, "There are around twenty. We don't know them personally, but *everyone* here knows who they are."

Homicide is almost nonexistent in Bhutan, but other dangers lurk. Seatbelts aren't required by law, so infants and toddlers are often spotted passing by while held on laps in the front seat. Unlike kids from LA being treated like mini–Dalai Lamas, here excess faith seems placed in fate.

With far less than a million citizens, Bhutan is the most expensive place to visit in the world (and therefore also one of the least visited), with each tourist having to pay $200 a day to enter. This fee was designed to create sustainable levels of tourism, but seems to have had the opposite effect

Master Yeshi has devoted his life to keeping zhungdra music alive and has won national awards for his original compositions.

with large hotels—some still in the midst of being built—found on almost every block, and almost all sitting empty.

During our three-night stay we did not see one other guest, yet there were staff milling everywhere.

The nation became even more desolate after COVID with around two hundred thousand citizens estimated to have fled for jobs, mostly young men, leaving behind seniors and women. Indian immigrants fill the bulk of the local, unskilled laborer roles as those south of the border do for the USA, Malawians in South Africa, and Albanians and Moroccans for Italy.

The most probable danger in Bhutan would be the police, not the criminals. With an absolute monarchy, the king possesses sovereign powers and any decision made by him is final.

Bhutan was the first carbon-neutral nation, with the only other being Suriname. Over 60 percent of Bhutan's land is mandated to remain forested. The omitted flip side of that is how much easier it is for countries to go eco if they were never overtaken for decades or centuries by industrialization and mass consumerism.

International airlines refuse to operate in Bhutan due to the hazards Paro Airport presents for landing. Therefore, the two national Bhutanese companies are the only way in. A sudden drop is required to arrive and a nearly vertical ascent to clear the ridge ahead after takeoff.

Down the street stood the "Karma Store." I wished they sold in bulk. And at the neighboring Cum Bar, it's highly unlikely they serve its mistaken namesake. As with everywhere else in the world, capitalism had found a way to warp and hijack meaning.

Classical music from Bhutan was established in 1616. Derived from Sanskrit, the language used in songs in the zhungdra style is indecipherable to most Bhutanese.

The tallest sitting Buddha in the world keeps watch from the hilltop.

We pitched camp in the forest on a mountain with no name, where the largest sitting Buddha in the world (169 feet tall) kept watch, the top of its head just clearing the ridgeline.

There were no closed-circuit cameras. Only the trees kept surveillance. But some cops did suspiciously appear on the road below within minutes of our arrival. They loitered for hours, keeping me on edge. Thankfully they left without interfering.

Holding hardened yak cheese cubes in their cheeks for stamina, the musicians were mostly shy. They inched farther and farther away from the mics after each song, requiring the stands to be continually reset.

I've learned the hard way that looking directly at musicians makes them grow self-conscious, fearing that something is wrong. Instead, it's better to use peripheral vision to check the mics, and, for the sake of one's own perceptual and mental functioning, remembering to always look up at the sky, at least once—even if only for a few seconds—is indispensable.

Fighting the rain each day, one microphone expired in the line of duty. Generally, a microphone tells the truth, while effects distort or disguise it. Once, I mistook that the equipment had gone kaputt and dreaded that an afternoon's recording was doomed. Only later on review did I decipher that the singer had been unintentionally "throat singing" with a natural wow flutter in her voice.

Though there was much noise from the road below, the forest floor acted as a sound absorber. Proximity is vital to intimacy. Aside from abrupt, transient sounds like coughs, strikes, and scrapes, each microphone largely only gleans whatever is closest rather than loudest.

And when each song was through, the crows appeared in droves, chiming in—more loudly for some performances than others as if critiquing each piece.

The first day, the rain forced us to take shelter in a local recording studio. We ended up sequestered in a dull, windowless, sonically dead room with no need to touch one piece of the equipment there. A descent from high altitude Blue Pines to fluorescent lights and walls covered in egg-crate foam, simply to have a roof overhead. I'd traveled halfway around the world only to finish precisely in the kind of space I ardently avoid—sentenced to an auditory purgatory.

I genuinely prefer recording outdoors. One of the reasons is elemental: oxygen. It's hard *not* to make something artificial in an artificial environment, saturated in electromagnetic fields (i.e., a dim, sound-proofed "isolation booth").

Record engineering is similar to cinematography. The choices as to what sounds and colors are emphasized influence the audience's perception but tend to work best when they're subtle or subliminal rather than heavy-handed. The difference with live recording is that the immediate atmosphere tends to make these determinations indelibly at the very instant the performance occurs.

In the end, though, the methods don't really matter. The quest to even occasionally reach transcendent musical minutes—through whatever route possible—is all that is ultimately of consequence.

The final day, a drizzle began to fall again as a young woman, Tshechu, sang. It was picturesque, but each time a lone raindrop hit any microphone, it sounded like a bomb had been detonated in the headphones.

Recording is rarely a neutral process. Performances tend to sound better or worse when played back, usually moving in opposition to how they were perceived in real time. Thrilling sections falling flat or seemingly flaccid ones revealing a marked intensity blunted when heard live.

Throughout history so many gold standard recordings have been aesthetic accidents, resulting from the technical limitations or debilitation of the equipment used.

Despite having the wonderful woodlands as an impromptu amphitheater, Bhutan was far from Zen-like. At night we were kept awake by discothèques, feuding stray dog packs, and religious chants predawn.

When I inquired if any tourists might appear or interfere at our hillside location, our friend Mangal stated, "I'm not sure there are any right now." His conviction was that we were the only tourists in the entire nation. As it turned out, we did not see another foreign visitor during our days there, save for a smattering on the plane out.

While the bourgeois visitors that do come partake of suites that can run as much as $5,000 a night to play out their *Eat Pray Love* enlightenment experience, many locals in the city defecate in ceramic holes on the bathroom floor and flush with buckets.

The countless occasions that I meet people around the world who've taught themself to speak English well, I am in awe. I don't demand or expect this ability. I am humbled by it and ashamed of my own lack of fluency in languages other than my own.

In compensation, I try to tune into differing cultural rhythms—how long eye contact is held, the pace of movement and turns, the rate of reply, the way couples and families in dispute walk untethered as they near the point of fracture or when the full independence for adolescents nears.

Zhungdra music features extended vocal tones that weave labyrinthian patterns, cumulatively decorating melodies with minimal instrumental accompaniment. As with so much folk music around the world, it often bares mournfully bent notes. At moments, listeners may close their eyes and think they've drifted to the Mississippi Delta. But similarly, a Bhutanese could stumble into a Beale Street bar and be transported back to Thimphu. Some of the bluesiest music I've ever heard was in Bhutan.

But like all musical forms, certain licks and riffs recur—be they hammered-on seconds, stutter beats, or rockabilly hiccups.

One of the benefits of learning a melodic instrument like the primary ones used by these artists—the drum-nyen (a lute with three double strings) and the chiwang (a two-string, bowed fiddle)—is that it connects you physically to the music since you are not triggering a preexisting sound, but adjusting your body to produce a new one. No matter how much one may contort with a computer keypad or how hard you hit, the sounds remains unchanged. With a physical instrument, your neurological system becomes wired with intervals and rhythms, so that even in the absence of the instrument, your hands, arms, and fingers remain musically sensitized and activated, due to the sonic elements having entered your body more fully.

Far from a "small" country, mountainous areas compose the bulk of Bhutan's land surface. If their countless folds and valleys were stretched flat, they'd likely quadruple the span of Bhutan's national borders in all directions. Many singers had come from remote villages which required over two days' journey to sing songs like "Even If You Long for the Home You Left, You Must Remember Where You Are Now." As is frequently the case with gifted rural artists, many were not literate, had never gone to school, and signed with an X.

Despite diligence and good intentions, often there is a strug-gle with ensuring accurate translations. One elder changed the spelling of his name three times in three days, and in the end it turned out legally that he only had one name to begin with (since he had no first name at all) regardless of his having consistently provided a first and last name.

These were the antithesis of overeager customer-ser-vice singers that plague heavily commercialized cultures. Only one person veered into being performative. I sadly

Zeko sings from beneath the power lines.

learned long ago that the people I might most enjoy having a coffee with do not necessarily make for the best work colleagues, and that instead the strongest artistic partners teeter toward unlikability and often just don't seem to give a fuck.

But here was yet another case of the most bashful singer prevailing. Dorji's voice so soft when speaking it was nearly inaudible, but he had an entire textural spectrum bottled up discreetly inside.

As always, we actively sought out elders and women. Nonetheless, the oldest person that participated was sixty-one and few of the fifteen singers had even made forty.

The irony of youth worship is that being young is not an accomplishment. Becoming older, enduring, and having done something even semimeaningful with your life is.

Only one woman, Lemo, accompanied herself. She played the yangqin hammered dulcimer, which sent the birds berserk. But as with everywhere on earth, animals are almost never out of tune or arhythmic—instead, they are close listeners responding.

The other women worked chorally. Whether duos, trios, quartets, or more, they devised a way to make space for every voice. But one elder's song was so rare that none of the others could join her, never having heard it. They gave us a hand-woven rug utilizing geometric patterns remarkably like those associated with Peru.

In the end, universal power dynamics played out. A group leader kept interfering with the artists, goading them to perform "correctly." But these disturbances had the opposite of their intended impact—the singers became more hesitant and fettered, shifting into their heads over their hearts, their trust in self undermined.

9

Taa

Our Language May Be Dying, but Our Voices Remain

The Taa language in Botswana possesses 112 sounds, the most of any language in the world—including many "click consonants" made with the teeth and tongue. In contrast, English has approximately 44 sounds, Italian 32. There are only around 2,500 Taa speakers remaining and the language is dying.

Botswana is a diamond-drunk nation, hosting the biggest diamond mine on earth. But the Taa villages at the farthest reach of dead-end dirt roads are where the country expires and the people are left forgotten by unguarded borders. One village's name literally translates to "the very end."

Wherever we reached, elderly shamans—two who were blind—gathered and played spectral ballads. They told us that there were many other songs that they knew, but those could not be sung since performing them in the daytime would bring bad luck.

Anywhere you go, pretty voices are as common as weeds. But when eighty-three-year-old Xhashe, opened his mouth, sound almost didn't come out, just feeling. As a rule: the higher the emotion versus volume quotient, the more depth to the singer.

One shaman's son said he hadn't heard this music performed since he was a child in the 1980s, almost forty years prior. Many were "homemade-beer-drinking songs."

Gonxlae sang with a weary
ease that runs counterpoint
to commercialized,
performative singers.

The explanation of lyrics often took far longer than the songs themselves—untranslatable, abstract thoughts encapsulated in single words. When people speak the same language, their ears are tuned to the same frequencies and structures of logic. They hear things others literally cannot.

One shaman's parents taught him to play the thumb piano as a way of remembering them after they'd gone.

Botswana is so flat, at sunset you can see the earth's own shadow—the horizon bending back on itself. We visited the highest point in the country, a mere hill that would barely register as even that elsewhere.

Near there sat the Kanye West exit—not named after the rapper, but in homage to the larger, adjoining town of Kanye.

The towns resembled trailer parks in America's southwest—not dissimilar to anywhere that housing lines railroad tracks. So much so, the towns could've easily passed for Barstow save for the Botswana ranchers riding bareback on donkeys. This is the land of the original cowboys, millennium before Columbus's mistaken navigations landed him on the outskirts of North America.

"We don't eat transport," locals intoned, referring to donkey and camel. Some donkeys pulled salvaged pickup truck beds as wagons.

It took an hour and a half to travel fifteen miles on a gravel road. The nearest school was forty miles in the opposite direction. Encircled in a chalky white dust cloud of our vehicle's own making, we didn't cross a soul for over an hour—just the occasional misspelled road sign, with local names anglicized. It was like being trapped in a rumbling time machine, progress forward not visible until we suddenly came to rest and an enclave emerged. The only person in the village with a high-school education acted as our mediator.

"The problem we have here is moonshine," one singer summarized.

Xhashe, an eighty-three-year-old shaman, reportedly
often takes solo walks in the desert for days.

This was clear by those prematurely aged from drinking spirits distilled from gasoline. One hunchbacked man
busted out a turtle dance on all fours. He looked well into
his seventies but shockingly was only thirty-six years old.

Hearing of a hundred people killed in a militant attack
up north, they shrugged. That many had died from COVID
in their village of a thousand.

All this in buckshot of a game reserve—rumored to
harbor a clandestine diamond mine—where hunters cross
an ocean to spend small fortunes to kill for sport.

A local man kept trying to sell us a homemade bow and
arrow, seemingly more as a warning than a sincere attempt
at salesmanship.

As we loaded up to leave, the town schizophrenic came
begging, grabbed my sleeve, and tracked me as I circled the
car. It felt oddly familiar, hearkening back to my psych ward
worker days decades earlier.

The driver from the city was rattled by this, especially when our car was partially surrounded and blocked as he gingerly backed away. But we made it safely on our way. Every culture has its own version of macho. Maybe softer and askew, but nonetheless toxic and sinister.

And as so often is the case when searching for music, an elderly man had only remembered that his wife was a singer as an afterthought while we were leaving.

I dozed off in the car on the way back while, over the radio, accordion music played cat and mouse with the static. The region's kissing cousin to Tejano, this accordion genre is what happened when German immigrants went south rather than all the way west to Texas, bringing along their drunken polkas.

The local man from the capital driving with us was vexed to discover that there was such poverty in his country. In his thirties and well traveled, he'd never known this side of his nation and couldn't stop talking about it for days—more to himself than us.

In the Kalahari desert, there are prehistoric cave paintings at a spot where some believe the creation of the world began. During the late nineteenth century, the unfenced land of the nomadic people appeared unclaimed to colonialists, so they laid stakes posthaste.

But the villages where we recorded existed before the nation.

As a straight, white male raised in a violent, winner-takes-all system, I know that anywhere I go, I am the savage. This is a role-reversed "civilizing mission"—any transgression or deficiency is my own. For it is I who am the other.

In Botswana's capital, Gaborone, low-rise complexes have been erected on empty lots that were under threat of seizure if landowners did not adhere to government mandates to develop. After the country gained independence in 1964, the capital city was hatched almost from scratch, wasteland turned corporate. It lacked the history of the colonial commercial center, Francistown. And that is exactly why it was chosen. It was a clean slate.

At all hours, flatscreen TVs looped images for nightclubs that had more promoters outside than customers. Inside, DJs blasted beats that in a blind taste test could be from anywhere. Decked out in suit and tie but smelling of campfire, a man asked me where the "69"—slang for toilet—was. With Botswana having had one of the highest AIDS rates worldwide, condoms are supplied gratis at every hotel bedside. Here reality long ago surpassed piety.

Daycare centers have popped up all over the city, due to a combination of mothers increasingly working outside the home and a generation of grandparents less willing to care for the young.

Recycled luxury cars flood the streets, a mistaken indicator of affluence. Botswana is a dumping ground for vehicles that were required to be taken off the streets in Japan due to that country's rigorous vehicle inspection system. Here BMWs and Mercedes can be snatched up for five figures.

Some Zimbabwean immigrants live in the sewage pipes. They follow the same ancient migratory paths as animals, which eases passage, but endangers the migrants further due to potential encounters with elephants and hippos.

Our local friend, Andy, reflected the multicultural nation. Each grandparent was from a different country—Zimbabwe, South Africa, the Congo, and only one from Botswana. He recollected how his grandmother was given a fake diamond as a retirement gift after decades slogging for an actual diamond mine.

When treating entire regions or people as monoliths, what's often ignored is that every place has migration. And not just those from other nations, but also internal shifting.

Tsaa played with gloved hands due to the winter cold that
blanketed the plains and rendered our breath visible.

Anyone moving from an agricultural area to an urban one,
or vice versa, will experience disorientation, and that is the
frisson which drives change.

In a rural, northern transit town, a young rap posse tried to
run off a group of kids who kept hanging around. The children's collective profile resembled a notched skyline—from
toddlers to preadolescents. I instead waved the youngsters
back and asked them to help provide handclaps. They
performed so exceptionally, it could shame a Hollywood
session percussionist.

Few things are quite as bittersweet as hearing young
men—their lives inflated with hope—declaring how much
they want to preserve their traditional culture while wearing Nike Airs.

As we recorded, we competed with roofers' hammering
and idling jeeps.

Across town, the white African landlord next door mocked the singers over the fence. Later, that singer recounted how a white teacher from South Africa had told him he didn't have a musical bone in his body. But he went on to master the marimba.

As residents sat on stripped car seats for front porch furniture, the female chief rolled-up in her 4×4. Falling midwinter south of the equator, the month of June translates to "don't go out at night." As the sun rose, our breath visibly interlaced while speaking with one another.

In contrast to tales of stealing or sneaking photographs of "primitives," while Marilena was taking photos of the artists, a neighbor we'd never met ran to change clothes, then climbed through the property's barbed-wire fence uninvited. She jumped into the frame, insisting that she be photographed, too. The sun was setting and the light glorious, but regardless the lush look, hers are photos we'd likely never use. It was too folkloric, anthropological, and unrelated to the focus of our recording—those who had actually sung or performed.

One neighbor thanked us. "Very few Americans come to Botswana except to kill something."

And then she schooled us about how scorpions with bigger talons have less venom. They kill with the claws. Therefore, the larger ones appear scarier, but it is the small ones who pack the most poison. They're the ones you have to look out for.

The name of the Taa language itself translates to "human being," making its threat of extinction even more poignant—the language living in the people, not on the page.

10

Comorian

All Passports Are
Not Created Equal

Most US citizens are accustomed to going just about anywhere they want in the world and being welcomed with open arms. The primary hurdle tends only to be shopping around for the cheapest airfare.

For citizens in lower resource countries, though, this rarely is the case. Governments in more prosperous nations erect nearly impassable bureaucratic hurdles to discourage those harboring "immigration intent" from crossing borders.

This inequity presents yet another negative factor toward non-English speaking musical artists being heard globally, an asymmetry that detrimentally impacts not only the arts, but also areas like business, athletics, science, and health care as well.

Over the past decade, the music projects that Marilena and I have done with rural artists from nations such as South Sudan, Rwanda, Cambodia, Suriname, and Malawi have led to twenty-two artists being able to leave their countries for the first time ever. But in almost every single instance, their visa applications have been rejected on the first attempt. Quite comically, in 2015 the South Sudan group Acholi Machon—whose repertoire features songs like "Acholi Land Is Good Land for Staying" in celebration of their nation having gained independence after a fifty-year civil war—were initially denied on the basis that there

M'madi plays a handmade Gambussi accompanied by
drummer D. Alimzé in an abandoned downtown theater.

was "no reason to believe you will return home following
your visit."

The Comorian duo were invited to perform at Peter
Gabriel's WOMAD Festival alongside such stars as the
Flaming Lips, Angélique Kidjo, and Brazilian legend Gilberto
Gil. Comorian's appearance reportedly would mark the first
time in WOMAD's forty-year history that musicians from
Comoros appeared at the festival.

But what ostensibly would seem conclusively good news,
for Comorian merely marked the beginning of a daunting
legal and logistical odyssey.

Comoros is an island nation off the southeast coast of Africa.
It has a population of only 850,000 people and the main

island, Grande Comore, is a meager 396 square miles (smaller than Rome, about a quarter larger than NYC).

Since the nation's independence from France in 1975, only six nations maintain embassies there: China, South Africa, France, Sudan Tanzania, and the United Arab Emirates. Thus, in order for a Comorian citizen to travel to most places on earth, they have to first travel to a third nation—such as Zimbabwe or Kenya—that host visa offices where Comorian citizens can apply. And these trips themselves usually require the Comorian citizen to first obtain a visa to travel to the intermediary nation in order to then apply for the necessary visa for the target country. Worse, the application process necessitates that the applicant must surrender their passport during the interim, a period which can last months. This then prevents the person from traveling home or other places internationally while their visa application is reviewed.

Contrast that with the USA, Canada, Australia, New Zealand, Japan, South Korea, and most European nations, all of whose citizens can travel to 165 or more countries visa-free or with visa-on-arrival options. The inequality radiates.

Such factors are far from trivialities as to why K-pop has reached the world in a way that music from most less endowed nations are almost invariably unable to. The most common response I've received when speaking about Comoros over the years—even from multiple "global music" experts—has dismayingly not just been, "Where is it?" but "*What* is it?"

Though the liberty to travel is guaranteed by Article 13 of the United Nations' declaration of human rights, these privileges are not universally shared. Becoming airborne is an extravagance that all but a handful of elite countries are not automatically nor easily granted.

Few airlines fly to Comoros and almost none do so daily. The officially recommended UK visa office for Comoros is in Mauritius, which sits just four island nations southeast of Comoros. But getting there requires taking three planes that are first routed to Ethiopia—far in the northeast of the African continent—then back down through South Africa where there is an almost ten-hour layover before heading back to the east. An overnight, twenty-five-hour journey whose flights are often more expensive than those to Europe.

The Comorian duo instead submitted their visas in Dar es Salaam—the biggest city of the neighboring mainland country, Tanzania. But Tanzania is a nation that neither man had ever visited before and where they do not speak any of the languages. Ultimately, Tanzania's office was chosen due to there being direct flights available.

Beyond the thousands of dollars in costs just to apply for a visa to perform a single show in the UK (in what was to be a mere four-day visit), the payment process itself is fraught with impediments: though the application itself can be paid with a credit card, the private-company interview appointment services can only be paid via bank wire. Meanwhile, the local flight could only be booked in cash at the local airport.

Comorian's application involved sixty-six pages of documents. And although both members were fully vaccinated against COVID, the Comorian COVID certificates did not feature a QR code. Therefore, the men were required to get not only a PCR test to go to Tanzania but also a second test for them to board the one-hour flight to return to their own country—the government that had issued their vaccination status.

The process for citizens from the USA and every country in the world if traveling to Comoros? You just show up, fill out a few lines of data on a postcard, pay thirty dollars, and you're in. Yet another trade deficit in our global economy.

Soubi and M'madi triumph onstage in the United Kingdom.

The two members of Comorian, M'madi Djibaba, fifty-nine, and Soubi Attoumane, sixty-nine, are not only masterful musicians but instrument builders—a tradition that sadly is dying on the islands.

As Soubi laments, "The young people now just want to go out and buy an instrument. That is, if they are even interested in playing at all." Attoumane is one of the last living players of the gambussi, a long-necked lute.

M'madi specializes in the ndzendze—a two-sided box "guitar." His uses fishing line for strings, and being a welder by trade, he has added tuning pegs to what is customarily a fixed-pitch instrument.

Soubi looks
heavenward.

"I just want to share my music with the world and cele-brate my country. I would never leave Comoros. I don't need to travel to know how beautiful and blessed Comoros is. Comoros is my home. I am proud to be Comorian. I would never want to live anywhere else," stated M'madi.

The two musicians' visas were approved mere days prior to their flight and only because of pressure applied from within the government. Nonetheless, the musicians receiving the passports back in time remained a question mark. Express shipping between Comoros and Tanzania had proven to take five days, at best.

Worse, since the men were required to give up their passports during the months their applications' were reviewed, M'madi and Soubi were caught in the catch-22 of not being able to travel internationally back to Tanzania to collect the documents once approved. Fortunately, a friend with a passport was willing to travel to Tanzania on their behalf. But he had to fly on the last available direct flight that could arrive in time and then wait without guarantee for days at a hotel around the corner from the visa office in the hope that the passports would then show up.

Any time that I board a plane or wait in an airport security queue, I cannot help but think of these individuals—and the far too many other such cases that I've witnessed. What seem to me annoyances are, in fact, privileges. Privileges that the majority are vigorously denied, ones that I have in no way earned.

As further evidence of systemic disparity, rather than posing an imminent, credible threat, Comoros, has never had a mass shooting reported, nor virtually any terrorist attacks or activity. Yet during that same year millions of Americans visited Europe, visa-free, while the USA averaged almost two mass shootings per day.

Standing in the middle of the street,
Soubi welcomes a rainstorm.

As employed senior citizens who are homeowners and are long married with multiple children and who speak no English, neither Soubi nor M'madi fit any aspect of the profile for an "aspiring immigrant" who might overstay a visa. Those posing such risks are generally single males in their teens or twenties. It's hard to imagine a gray-haired, good-natured, white father with no criminal history attempting to travel *anywhere* and *ever* being subjected to the same scrutiny that Soubi and M'madi suffered. And if such a thing did occur, it would likely go viral.

In an era where greater inclusiveness and diversity are claimed, systemic exclusion continues virtually unabated—cloaked by the red tape of oracle administrative systems.

This sadly familiar incident brings into focus how many various factors intersect and prevent artists from smaller and less-advantaged nations like Comoros being celebrated abroad. Even when the rare invitation is ever granted, the artists being able to seize that opportunity is routinely sabotaged and denied. The answer to the mystery of why, for decades, no artist from Comoros ever appeared at the WOMAD festival is evident—not for want of talent but an abundance of obstruction.

Ultimately, it is audiences that are cheated rather than protected by their own government's discriminatory practices.

Thankfully, the Comorian duo's visas did arrive one day before their departure and were then hand-carried back to them by their friend, Toimimou, with just hours to spare.

But such serendipity was not the case for some international musicians who were forced to cancel that year last-minute. Instead, select "World of Music, Arts and Dance" stages sat dark.

Their silence screamed.

11

Sainkho Namtchylak (Tuva)

Where Water Meets Water

Sainkho Namtchylak planned to return to Tuva, but then Russia invaded Ukraine, blocking her from her homeland.

We instead recorded throughout the abandoned islands of Venice, the places discarded amid tourism's gold rush. Venice's lagoon covers an area equivalent to Chicago, and the waters are littered with historical debris. The cluster of islands that most people think of as "Venice" sits at the center of the lagoon dividing north and south, and makes up only a tiny portion of the greater area.

In defiance of the "visual album" trend, where image often carries more weight than sound, the goal of this project was to create an "audio film," indelibly imbued by time and place, where sounds carry the story.

One track was recorded on the most haunted island in Venice, a spot that many claim is the most haunted place on earth. An estimated 160,000 people died there, and rumors run that over 50 percent of the soil is made of human ash. A psychiatrist who conducted brain surgery experiments on patients ultimately committed suicide by throwing himself from atop the belltower. Sainkho's seven octave voice can be heard bouncing off the walls of the former asylum, creating an otherworldly reverb.

During another song, a search-and-rescue mission helicopter hovered overhead, extracting victims from the

Sainkho records on the asylum island that is allegedly one of the most haunted places on earth.

sea as we recorded on the fortress rooftop where Venetians had managed to sink one of Napoleon's ships during his army's takeover.

The songs themselves tend to tell you what an album will be. With 100 percent live, improvisatory performances there are moments where things congeal palpably, and others where they fall apart. My goal is to always show people in the best possible light, to honor them. Single-take, live recording always involves an act of mutual, blind trust between producer and artist.

Sainkho speaks four languages (Tuvan, Russian, English, German) but chose to sing phonetically here in the "language of nature."

Another ultimately unused tune was tracked while riding through the canals of Venice at night in a gondola, the only accompaniment the sound of the oar and couples whispering (or drunkenly yelling) at bridge crossings. This entire album is a celebration of simultaneity—the main accompaniment, water.

Sainkho is one of the rare female throat singers. Initially tutored by her grandmother, Sainkho has battled misogyny and released almost fifty albums, all the while skirting the edge of poverty to practice her art.

She only became a professional singer by chance due to the Communist Party banishing musicians and artists to Tuva. As most do, that social engineering plan backfired and led to the creation of new pockets of bohemia and rebellion in the formerly isolated regions of the republic. As a result, she met her husband—an older jazz bassist from Moscow—and this altered the course of her life.

The city of Venice is sinking less from tides than from tourism. The residential population has dwindled from a high of 164,000 in 1931 to now fewer than 50,000 people. The visitors outnumber the locals most days by three to one. This is the equivalent of thirty million people invading Bangkok daily. Instead, far less than that many people in a year visit Bangkok, even though it is the world's most-visited place. It's a matter of proportion. Though Bangkok receives over twenty million visitors annually, that averages nonetheless to the residents still outnumbering the travelers daily, 171 to 1.

Airbnb has colonized Venezia, particularly suited to capitalize on Italy's having dropped in mere decades from having one of the highest birth rates in the world to among the lowest. Thus, the current generation of Italians has experienced a windfall of inheritance. Instead of a single home being fought over and subdivided between numerous siblings and cousins—as until very recently was commonly the case—now Italians often inherit not only property but *properties*. Frequently, this is from childless aunts and uncles that they barely knew and in a town they've never visited, have no commitment to, and even despise as a playground for foreigners.

For the first time now there are more beds for visitors than citizens in Venice. This is what happens when you commercialize residential neighborhoods.

Sightseers block narrow bridges with selfie sticks as inhabitants dodge and weave, attempting to navigate their way to school or the doctor through the hordes. Bridal "hen parties" wave colossal silicone dildos as children pass, and later drunkenly ask where the "exit" is, as if the community were an amusement park. Venice has increasingly become more like living in an airport than a community—a place of transit. Like Las Vegas but with better buildings. I know this because I am a resident. And I've run this manic obstacle course for over a decade.

Despite Sainkho having stayed at the same Grand Canal hotel for a week, on the final night the hotel clerk denied Sainkho entry to her room after dark because her name was not the primary one on the reservation—a racially driven hazing that no sixty-five-year-old white Italian signora

The primary accompaniment on Sainkho's latest album: water.

would ever be subjected to. A shameful reminder of Italy's repressed colonial past.

Obscured by Italy's cobblestone city centers, fine art, and scenic beauty, the nation's negative history regarding race and xenophobia is often hidden. During the renaissance, young African children referred to as *Mori* ("dark ones") were often used as household slaves in Venice and their faces continue to decorate many doorknobs throughout the city. During WWII, an estimated 7,680 Jewish citizens of Italy were killed due Mussolini's complicity with the Nazis. Yet in 2008 Italy's prime minister, Silvio Berlusconi, professed that Mussolini had merely sent people on "holiday" and in 2013 Berlusconi even praised Mussolini at a Holocaust Memorial Day event.

In recent years, Italy's first Black governmental minister, Cécile Kyenge, and Italian born and raised soccer star, Mario Balotelli, have both had racists hurl bananas at them in public. In 2021, the national television network, RAI, refused to officially ban blackface following an uproar over degrading impersonations of Beyoncé and other musicians. Also in 2021, a model turned television host mimicked Asian stereotypes—making slanted-eye gestures on the air—and then issued the hollow, stock apology days afterward that she was "the furthest thing from a racist." She has remained with the program since.

Privilege only ends when people stop believing that they're doing someone else a favor simply by not overtly treating them poorly.

No one makes music in a vacuum. But the most original artists like Sainkho have influences that are not usually obvious or apparent. Often culture arrives obliquely. Their way of hearing is different from ours. They can listen to the same material as millions of others but still take away something entirely different.

For one final song, Sainkho sang *to* the Adriatic Sea. A sunburned middle-aged snorkeler, bothered by our presence, sat sullenly at the end of the otherwise empty breakwater pier. Like a toddler, he stamped the heels of his fins against the rocks in protest, unwilling to recognize this unforeseen treasure he'd found just above the ocean's surface.

12

Africatown, AL

Ancestor Sounds

The rental car clerk at the airport seemed surprised that we were there: "People don't usually come to Mobile unless they *have* to."

Tule fog blanketed the roadways as we entered by night a city emptied in New Year's Eve's aftermath, creating a sense of nonarrival—as if we might've landed in the wrong locale entirely.

Carnival originated stateside in Mobile before being claimed and popularized by New Orleans, and the last slave trading market is now home to Alabama Power & Electric. Even with many monuments coming down, the South remains a place where losers rather than victors are held up as heroes—the Confederate statues erected and streets named as a nonsurrender, a lingering desire to rise again by the racist "dickweed" underbelly.

In Africatown, the headstones all face east—toward "home" (i.e., Africa). And "homegoing" remains the name locally for funerals. Many Buffalo Soldiers are buried there also. The Africatown community was founded by freed slaves from the Clotilda, the last slave ship that entered America—illegally and a mere three years before the Emancipation Proclamation. An ancestor reportedly wanted everyone to learn to pronounce his name correctly so that if they ever met another person from Africa, that person would know

Africatown has been surrounded from all
sides by environmental invaders.

who was being spoken of. And the first thing he did when he
was freed was build a drum, an outlawed act under slavery.

Years before, in rural northern Ghana, I was struck
when spotting a hand-painted "Alabama Barbershop" sign.
Echoing this connection, in Mobile, a local blues musician
played a kologo from the Ghanaian region, a guitarlike
instrument he knew by another name.

Fumes pour from a smokestack in the community whose citizens have suffered a disproportionately high rate of cancer.

City governments divide and conquer with roads and zoning—freeways fracturing neighborhoods. Strolling with my six-year-old daughter along an expressway without sidewalks as semis thunder past, manifested viscerally these streets' divisiveness.

On the edge of a residential Africatown street, a corporation built a factory illegally, but were reportedly only fined $5,000 and allowed to remain. That factory's sounds fill the air at all hours, making recording there a near impossibility. While I walked the neighborhood, my lungs were overcome from those fumes filling a cul-de-sac of condemned and collapsed roof homes. Throughout the streets, empty lots told the story. One of absence.

The ratio of pit bulls to people skyrocketed in the pockets where it grew difficult to distinguish abandoned houses from those occupied.

The Africatown Bridge takes its name from a population that has largely been scattered due to the forces of redevelopment.

Gentrification doesn't really force people out of a city, but onto the street. They return or continue to live in the same city, but under unlivable conditions.

Municipalities conserve Civil War fortresses, but tear down housing projects.

On the heels of recent attention toward Africatown, the burgeoning tourist industry was palpable—locals rolled up in cars offering "tours." When asked if she was a descendant, one local elder stated, "Maybe. I don't know," which is probably as close to the truth as could be found for many who grew up in the immediate area.

The sign of a local Baptist chapel read that all were welcome, but upon my arrival the music immediately halted and my greeting was met with silence. A man twice my width and depth, and half my age rose from the organ and charged, insisting I walk with him outside. Despite my attempt at a meek and nonthreatening entry, it was clear that all the downcast eyes and rolled shoulders in the world could not dampen a white man entering a Black southern church from being an understandably unwelcome sight.

Contrastingly, a local elder, Carla, tracked me, sidling by in her car and offering to sing. She let loose about as raw a vocal take as could be found, a lifetime of emotion unleashed in seconds.

One teenager, going by the handle "Rapper A," hopped into the passenger seat and freestyled a rap in our makeshift isolation booth on wheels. Most were people who said they were moved to participate—often choosing to do so anonymously—due to feeling that their voices had been left out of the mainstream historical reportage on the area.

Meant as an impressionistic document, rather than a definitive historical account, the outdoor nature of the recordings graphically renders the encroaching and ominous industrial sounds, documenting the environmental racism that plagues the neighborhood.

A local jazz musician, Joe Lewis, born in 1936, described how the old-timers had already stopped playing music when he was a child due to the introduction of Victrola radios. But for those who did play, the blues instrument of choice at the time became upright pianos baring broken keys after being discarded in droves by the monied following mass media's infiltration. Consequently, Mr. Lewis learned to play around the missing notes.

While I stopped to record grating mechanized sounds bellowing from another plant that floods the neighborhood with foul emissions, guards appeared in minutes, ushering me away.

The people have dispersed, but the factories remain. Rather than sending SOS signals, their smokestacks obscure them.

13

Yanna Momina

1947-2023

The planes strung like Christmas lights,
make their descent.
They keep coming,
but you'll never be back again.

I am heartbroken to write of the death of Yanna Momina
Abass at age seventy-six. Momina had been scheduled to
perform at 2023's WOMAD Festival but fell ill in the spring.
It was the hope that after surgery she would be well enough
to make the trip the next summer. Though this served as
a source of hope for her, the reports of her condition were
very grim.

Yanna sang in the Afar language, a nomadic, minority
population in Djibouti, whose region is also split between
two other nations (Ethiopia and Eritrea). Momina lived
rurally in the desert without electricity or running water.
In the absence of television, she prided herself on playing
music "for entertainment at night, not for money."

Sadly, this is yet another obituary I've had to draft.
Cambodia's Soun San (Khmer Rouge Survivors) and northern Ghana's "Small" Mbabila (fra fra) met eerily similar fates
in 2017 and 2022—both passing just as a trip out of their
country for the first time ever was imminent.

Yanna commands the edge of the Red Sea.

The first recording device is the mind. With recording we can time travel. When we listen to songs from our past, they reignite and animate the same parts of our brain used in the past, simulating who we were at the time. The same thing can happen when we see old friends or family members after a long time. It is a temporary regression of sorts.

With loved ones, their voices remain in our heads—a final echoing before evaporating entirely.

Featuring defiant and brash titles like "My Family Won't Let Me Marry the Man I Love (I Am Forced to Wed My Uncle)," Momina was revered within the culture for being one of the rare women who wrote her own songs. With her one-of-a-kind voice, Yanna specialized in a sort of daredevil vibrato singing, skirting the edge of chaos, but somehow always retaining control. Her voice was so strong that her songs—though frequently epic in length—thrived on the minimalist of accompaniment, often performed entirely a cappella.

We recorded her album in a raised stilt-hut on the edge of the Red Sea. The tide rushed in, unexpectedly surrounding us as seagulls circled—chattering and enlivened by the waves and the sound of Yanna's voice.

What I'll miss most about her, though, was her searing stare and vivacious laugh—knowing, but joyful no matter what the obstacles she faced in this life.

Bhakh singer Romalo
Ram drove three
and a half hours
through mountains
and mudslides after
having performed
at a wedding
until dawn.

14

Romalo Ram

Kashmir Tears: Don't Fear the People; Fear the Road Between

Kashmir is the region where three nuclear superpowers meet (out of only nine on earth): Pakistan, China, and India, with the powder keg Afghanistan thrown in for good measure along the border as a wild card. Fortunately, serving as a formidable deterrent to combat, our planet's highest mountains stand between China and India, which are also the world's two most populous nations.

In the land that gave the world cashmere blanket comfort, the government warning was to not leave the city limits of Jammu and particularly not to get within many miles of the Pakistan border due to terrorist activity. But we sat only fifteen miles from that border.

The rub with official travel advisories is that often they are based on outdated data. Once a place is flagged, it can be a near impossible process for it to become unmarked. No government official wants to be the one who lifted a restriction prematurely. Thus, as so frequently occurs with bureaucracies, the default is paralysis.

Though India is so often the stand-in for "exotic" frenzy in Hollywood films, for us it felt quite humdrum compared to places like South Sudan during its first year, where the knife-edge energy felt utterly unhinged.

There is inevitably a developmental pressure as nations convert from agricultural to urban life, people pushing up against the edges of rigid order and sharp corners, disobeying lines and colliding into each other's personal space. Literally driving outside the lanes.

But what appears chaotic to an outsider always has its own internal logic and flow.

In many ways, Jammu city seemed reminiscent of American stereotypes of Italian culture that rose during post-WWII Italy before their "economic miracle" occurred, stereotypes that have lingered, though long outdated. Having lived in Italy for more than a decade, if I had to find one word to describe northern Italians it would be aloof (and even a bit uptight)—far from the effusive, warm, and "colorful" way Italians are perpetually portrayed.

The ethnic regional tensions in the disputed state of Kashmir played out with a boss from the capital at the last minute undermining the arrangements we'd made months in advance. So we were forced to arrive blindly and start over from scratch. Fortunately, we found a sympathetic local, and the recordings came together quite quickly after all.

Reportedly, over 7,000 police, 20,000 military, and 20,000 civilians have lost their life to the separatist conflict in the region, and another 3,400 have gone disappeared. Widespread rape and other abuses are alleged, such as military members tying a civilian to the grill of their truck to discourage others from hurling stones at the vehicle as they patrolled.

Conflict zones can often be read in the faces of the community—a high concentration of unfixed, broken noses and deep facial scars remain as forensic evidence of daily life being a battleground. Nonetheless, across the street from where we stayed, "posh coaching" classes were offered.

Western world hippies have used India as their spiritual playground for generations, but Kashmir remains a more isolated place. We spotted only one person of obvious European descent over the course of almost a week, and encountered scant few fluent English speakers, even though it is one of the country's two official languages. Yet, the streets sported a plethora of ethnic and interpersonal diversity.

Even with more than a billion citizens, certain concentrations of affect—be it stoicism, rage, or joy—often become patterned and seep into the culture of a place, emotional elements that've been transmitted for generations and can't be fully excised, only reduced or magnified.

At the hotel, more bedroom doors were left open than closed—indication of a more communal lifestyle, even among the well-heeled. The lobby looped instrumental "playback music," like being stuck in a 1970s local news broadcast that never actually launches.

What terrorist attacks have occurred of late tend to be directed toward individuals who've emigrated from other parts of India and are seen as stealing jobs and diluting culture.

An upper-caste Indian singer I know married a tech billionaire but devoid of nuance and any seeming self-awareness bemoaned her plight as a "brown girl." Suffering is not a competitive sport. No one can know someone else's personal plight, particularly a straight, white male. But those whose stories are most often overshadowed are the poor, the people who have an intersectionality of factors compounding and amplifying one another negatively. I've repeatedly seen my own wife and daughter subjected to mistreatment for both being too dark *and* not dark enough. But more often I've seen them be celebrated in disparate regions for having a color close to the majority of people on earth—something other than white. But an even more universal discrimination than skin color is class and cash.

The Dogri language possesses over one million native speakers, yet they remain a minority, with Dogri spoken by less than 0.02 percent of the people in India. Dogri is

As with so many folk musicians in the world, it's a family affair. Romalo Ram, sings with his daughter, Sars.

the rare Indo-European language that is tonal. Though all languages use pitch to emphasize, emote, and contrast, few use pitch to convey literal meaning.

Following the ancient Hindu principle of nonviolence, in India cow slaughter is illegal in every region but one. Consequently, the country has the lowest rate of meat consumption on earth and has more vegetarians than the rest of the world combined. Since cows rule city streets—nonchalantly sauntering through traffic—the term "cow town" takes on an entirely different meaning here. Certainly, if one were reborn a cow, India would be a dream destination.

At the airport, security is tight—much like other heavily policed states such as Rwanda or Israel. Our bags were X-rayed five times and passports checked seven times (including while merely crossing the thirty yard gangway between the boarding gate and the plane itself).

Once in the air, though, the stewards' main role was crowd control—a nonstop game of Whac-A-Mole with passengers refusing to stay seated.

The night before, Romalo Ram and his band had performed for seven hours until dawn and then drove three and a half hours through rain and rockslides to meet us.

"We must sing at each wedding for as long as the people want us to. If they want more, we are obligated to keep going until whenever they decide they are ready to stop."

All seven members work as farmers in the mountains and one is also a mason. The hotel staff suggested that the band change clothes in the bathroom, something the group took as a personal insult. Many of the machine-gun-wielding military guards out front openly expressed their disdain toward the musicians. I was forced to book an extra room to use for only a few hours just so that Romalo and company could dress comfortably.

Romalo stated, "I'm so happy that someone is interested in Dogri culture. I have dreamed of this day. Please don't forget us. You are a person that respects the artists. I could see that in you immediately."

Every time I thanked him, he would instead refuse my gratitude, bow, and offer me even greater thanks.

The group recorded epic, call-and-response, a cappella numbers, with each generally nearing the ten-minute mark. The form is called "bhakh" and features the voices circling one another microtonally on long, held out, high notes. Romalo's claim to fame is adding colors such as humming and clucking that provide access points for audiences to this ancient folk music. Romalo even "invented" Dogri rap more than twenty years prior. Some tunes were battle songs, designed as back-and-forths between two crews where audiences egg the groups on until a winner is chosen between them.

Rinku Kumas is a blind singer who busks Dogri folk songs by the lake.

As much as I love working with first-time, "amateur" singers, true virtuosity like Romalo's is a similar joy. Both share an effortlessness.

Close harmony choral singing is found across alpine regions, from Appalachia to eastern Europe to northern India. It's as if the lower oxygen rate at high altitudes induces some hallucinatory effect globally.

Locals urged that we go "see the sights." But we knew nothing could be more inspirational or impressive than having met such gifted and uniquely specialized artists.

Fulfilling a pattern from time immemorial, Rinku Kumas is a blind, solo busker with crystal vocal tone—a Himalayan example of the Ray Charles phenomenon where the loss or diminishment of one sense results in the heightening of others. Rinku usually plays tambourine as he sings regional pop hits, but showed up on this occasion with an uninvited guitarist to accompany. This was a classic case of the local who was assisting overinterpreting our wishes and trying to provide what he *thought* we wanted rather than what we'd specified. The young guitar player broke into standard I/IV/V barre chords beloved by hobbyists around the world, straightening out the song's contours. But Kumas's music is best served unadorned, and even better a cappella.

Thus, I was abandoned to record with a blind man who did not speak English and then again on a busy street as we took photos and a crowd of onlookers quickly formed. This was another scenario where the decade-plus that I'd toiled in psychiatric emergency jobs and having grown up with a sister who was mostly nonverbal came into play. Somehow Kumas and I found a way to communicate—tactilely and sonically—navigating racing rickshaws, motorbikes, potholes, and mud puddles. As with most artists, I perceived my role as a copilot at best. It was he that was leading me.

To salve the ego of Kumas's would-be accompanist, we recorded the young player solo before we were through. He broke into an overwrought English-language version of Enrique Iglesias' already-overwrought song "Hero"— evidence of the cross-generational and cross-cultural damage a single, privileged commercialized family can inflict globally.

15

Himba Hymn (Namibia)

Skeleton Coast Ghosts

The Namib desert in southwestern Africa is the oldest and, thus, driest in the world.

We were headed to the far northwest, a mountainous region—"the place where you can see the rain," the moisture that so rarely graces the land. As a counterbalance to ethnocentric cliches, we'd come to record with possibly the most photographed people on earth, the Himba—to listen rather than gaze at them as if on display. To lend voice as an offset to their visual objectification.

The visitors we'd rode in with on the commercial jetliner were coming for the sights. We came for the sounds.

Sound-seeing.

Our objective is not to preserve anything but to inhabit the present day. Music resulting from a shared and lived moment. My intention is not to document but to create— sounds and songs that would not exist were it not for the meeting.

We had to stress multiple times that we did not want the musicians to don touristic tribal costumes. It was quite possibly the first music project in history that urged performers to cover up rather than pleading with them to expose more flesh. But it was to no avail. When the assigned hour arrived, the men all ditched the baseball caps and soccer jerseys they routinely wore. As for the women, almost

Kazongunbu looks down
from "the place where
you can see the rain."

without exception their torsos go bare, even in winter. We had to acquiesce. Forcing the issue would've only been another iteration of inauthenticity.

A few Himba locals catch occasional work in fake tribal villages, places where no one actually lives. Foreigners convene there to experience a minstrel song-and-dance, staged for their benefit.

"The tourists don't care if we sing. They just want us to dance," a sage elder somberly revealed.

The Himba have a rare tribal structure based on bilateral descent that helps them survive in one of the most extreme habitats on earth. Belonging to two clans—one from the mother, the other the father—enhances one's chances of survival in a hostile environment. At certain times, the Himba have been on the verge of elimination, particularly during the battle for independence in the 1980s when they collectively lost over 90 percent of their livestock.

Today, the Himba are placed under the jurisdiction of chiefs from other, more dominant tribes. Those outsiders make decisions on behalf of minority communities. In essence, authorities hold the Himba in secure camps against their consent to limit their wandering.

The Atlantic Ocean is a mere forty minutes away, but the government forbids them to visit the beach. Not unlike Indigenous people in the Americas and Australia (and beyond), the Himba have been corralled and cordoned— treated like trespassers on their own land.

It was here in 1904 that German colonizers committed their prototypical, pre-Holocaust genocidal experiment. An estimated 80 percent of the Himba people's linguistic cousins, the Herero, perished during that period.

Any time the driver asks you how to turn on the headlights or open the side window, it's time to take the wheel. I don't own a car and walk almost everywhere at home, but here I emergently faced twenty-six hours of driving, mostly off-road. Even more daunting, in Namibia they drive on the "wrong" side of the road.

This was the most lopsided travel to recording quotient we'd ever risked. Four days of flying plus four days of driving to record for only a few hours. Those three hours allotted were a make-or-break session. As a bonus, while I raced under deadline to return the 4×4 rental before sunset, I had to change a bellybutton-high tire in the midday sun.

Our local friend, Waka, had only been to the capital city, Windhoek, once in his life. It was his first experience with people not returning hellos.

I dismissed as some vestige of nineteenth-century anthropological fantasies the Himba people's renowned eyesight—heralded for its acuity and the identification of four primary colors rather than the usual three. That was until our local friend started spotting things on the side of the road a mile before they came into my view.

Dispelling pan-African fantasies, Waka said he'd never heard of the West African stars Angelique Kidjo, Youssou N'Dour, or even Fela Kuti. (Nor did he know the Beatles. But as always, a big nod to Michael Jackson.) As so often occurs, the most prominent Western musical influence was hymns—missionary hand-me-downs.

Our friend reported that the meanest tourists are locals descended from the Boers. One can see the Boers racism "from here"—all the way across the Pacific. Before ever reaching Namibian shores, history streaks the skies like distress flares. These were the apartheid people.

That said, five of the kindest and most thoughtful people I've ever met are white South African males, all unknown to one another. Extreme experiences are polarizing, and through the majority may adopt the negative as a model, there are those that channel such wickedness as a

The Himba men take
turns playing a rare and
cherished "cattle gun" horn.

Himba women have far too often been portrayed with a focus on their bare breasts, which is their customary daily dress.

reverse image—something to adamantly avert—like children of alcoholics living as teetotalers.

On the main highway, elephants provide job insurance for the locals, smashing national park, electrified iron fences as if they were balsa wood and requiring them to be repaired almost constantly. Left and right, giraffes and ostriches stood frozen like road markers.

The police checkpoints seemed setup to hassle the locals only. Tourists were waved through, granted a nearly automatic pass.

We only saw four bicycles while driving cross-country for four days. The evolution of travel modes mirrors capitalistic growth—from foot to bicycle to motorbike to compact car to oversized vehicles ultimately clogging previously clear passages.

From a distance, Namibian hitchhikers possess a stillness that yields trees, animals, and people almost indistinguishable—coexisting and harmonizing as one, aligned to a similar wavelength. When we rode even farther north from the city, it was telling how a child plugged his ears at a single truck passing. Here, noise was the exception.

Along the way, we spotted an "Out of Africa" restaurant, which seemed potentially less a welcome than a command. A Bank of Namibia sign had lost its letters to unintentionally proclaim "Ban Namibia." And the license plate abbreviation for Namibia, NAM, could send shockwaves through many Vietnam vets.

Living in the land of lions and hyenas, the scarce stray dog quickly grows humbled—a life spent with bowed head, tail between legs. Their bolder peers probably do exist, but don't last long—succumbing to almost instant natural selection.

In northern Namibia exists quite possibly the only place in the world where unaccompanied, topless young women feel safe hitching rides with strangers. In the supermarket, diversity and coexistence are on display as middle-aged Herero women with multicolored, flying nun hats and floor-length gowns shop for milk and maize, while passing without a glance half-naked youngsters in dreads, their skin lathered in clay.

Like with almost every project, there was the rock star—lacking in heart, brimming with ego. He'd shown up at our lodging, uninvited. An immaculate Bahama hat drawn low over his eyes, he refused to return my greeting for over a minute as he sat slouched in a chair while playing games on his phone. He was among the last people on earth I'd want to record. A chief's son, a prototypical nepo baby.

Once off the main two-lane, we passed only two cars on the road—one of those broken down, out of petrol. We crossed dried river beds that snake back on themselves throughout the valleys—gullies that flood in seconds during downpours.

Meanwhile, low-hanging clouds hovered like spacecraft and the multi-hued sky seemed the place where God would go to pray.

The low, round huts of the valley villages are so dispersed and sparse that the prime indicators of the existence of an enclave are the truck cabs sunk into the sand like cattle skulls.

No place I've ever visited is as thought or advertised. It's always more vibrant, bettering my imagination. We passed peaks and valleys that in America would be indelibly famous, but instead here in some cases remained unnamed.

Descending a pass, we crossed the clearcut line where towering termite sculpture mounds vanished from omnipresence—where the desert had grown too severe for wood to exist that the insects can feast on. It was the same spot where the cellphone coverage fractured for hundreds of miles in every direction.

There was an unexpected downpour as we arrived, and after what our local companion termed five hours of "African massage" courtesy of the bumpy ride, our first stop was to offer a vat of powdered coffee and sacks of sugar to the chief.

He told us, "We are so thankful that you would care and come all this way. It's unheard-of."

We were told there had been no fight in the village for over fifteen years. Nonetheless, all the men must carry a stick for self-protection, though the women are not allowed to unless elderly and in need of a cane for walking.

"We are all related. Peace is the only way," the chief concluded.

The next morning, a large group of singers had patiently amassed under a scattered group of trees outside of town.

They'd arrived days early, modeling forbearance.

We'd specifically expressed interest in hearing from elders. Evidencing the reduced life expectancy for men being around sixty years, their definition of elders amounted to people mostly younger than me.

A leader sang solo and exhibited one of the most objective measurements to a singer's immersion in a song. He began weeping as he praised friends who'd passed. His sorrowful, husky tenor was easily mistaken for another female's voice who possessed a raspy alto.

Through the use of live looping, psychedelic vocal tapestries were created as if snatched from the ever-shifting skies that enshrine the valley from all sides. But even more surreal results arose from members cupping hands over their mouth to create chorusing and flanging effects sans electricity.

As we stood in the midday sun, the wind wreaked havoc with the microphones. The energy peaked as thirty-one men and women of all ages broke into dance circle solos.

Rather than primitive or traditional, there was innovation, and timelessness, in their music making.

Mirroring other Western cultural excesses is the belabored way that we make music. Generally, the more writers or producers "teaming up" on a song, the hollower and blander the result. Contrastingly, musical traditions are rewritten by no one and everyone, tweaked and revised across centuries to fit the times. The true history of "tradition" is one of adaptation and progress rather than rigid adherence to precedent.

Musicians around the world tend to be outliers, if not drugged-out space cadets. Foreign "experts" often take the word of one local hippie as if it were gold, a gross act of overcompensatory and misplaced reverence. These erratic reports are then repeated as academic fact. Doing so is equal to someone documenting word-for-word the ramblings of a Deadhead on acid and taking that as Bible rather than nonsense.

A local protested that we were paying the singers "too much," since most have zero cash income at all. The majority exist solely by sustenance, with currency rarely playing a part in daily life. They survive based on what milk they can draw from their livestock and the crops that they can harvest when graced with precipitation. A choice few have coveted jobs at a campsite for foreigners that pass sporadically, but even those few make less than fifty US dollars a month. The Europeans who oversee it from afar hoard almost all the income generated.

Unlike the gangs of inflated gym boys on safari that spatter the countryside in the south, small children here have iron necks. Developed down deep at the base, they've been conditioned over a lifetime to carry weight on their head, to practice balance, grace, and patience—measured in days, years, generations, instead of seconds. A tolerance of time.

When we returned, the white rental car owner barked angrily at us. Unbeknownst to us, he'd been tracking our location by satellite all week and exclaimed, "Why did you take my car so far north? What were you doing up there? No one ever goes *there*.

"There? There is nothing."

16

The Good Ones

Rwanda ... You See Ghosts, I See Sky

The recordings of the Good Ones' latest and fourth album took place during the COVID lockdowns and in the wake of vocalist Janvier Havugimana unexpectedly becoming a grandfather for the first time. Like with the preceding three releases, it was recorded without overdubs on the group leader Adrien's hilltop farm—the same farm where Adrien and his children were born, the same land where he hid and survived the 1994 genocide.

Milk was in short supply for the newborn granddaughter. Far from poverty porn or pandering, this is just the daily reality of two incredibly gifted acoustic roots musicians who have been singing together for a lifetime.

No matter the group's international acclaim and opportunities to have performed in the UK, Europe, and the USA, the men and their family still struggle to make ends meet.

During these recordings, the cow and goat that Adrien was able to purchase because of the Good Ones' US tour did not interfere, but the newly installed and now-defunct electrical meter's beeping did. Later, as the wind swirled, farm tools took flight, freed from inertia for the length of a storm.

A neighbor passed in a tattered Rascal Flatts T-shirt, a trans-Atlantic castoff bearing a name that contained no meaning for him, beyond the protection the garment provided. He watched from afar before ambling on.

Adrien and Janvier have sung together since childhood, their voices entwining as one.

Though Janvier lives on the outskirts of the city, it is an almost impassable dirt road, with knee-deep ditches and bumps. His cellphone is frequently out of service, so communicating with him routinely requires having to physically go to his neighborhood and locate him. This can present a further challenge since his residence changes location often.

Despite the postgenocide safety of Rwanda being routinely touted, when visiting Janvier's area after dark, we were surrounded by local thugs who descended upon us, charging and bumping chests, and forcing us to negotiate a slippery escape from their posturing.

Adding to the obstacles the Good Ones face, what few instruments they possess have more than once been stolen from their homes during the rare times they venture out. Janvier was forced to compose songs for the next album in his head alone.

Adrien once told me how fascinating was the feel of his feet on concrete after arriving in London, his first trek outside of Rwanda. These men face multidimensional poverty. Beyond monetary deprivations, they've lacked access to education and basic infrastructure. As much as clean water, easily passable and reliable roads are often what is needed. Since voyages by water tend to be faster than going overland, historically it's often been easier in many senses to travel "around the world" than to the next rugged valley just around the corner. Intercontinental trade routes spanning and linking the globe have reenforced this selective connectivity and fragmentation for centuries.

The Good Ones laughed at how the trash-piled streets of New York were far dirtier than Kigali. And as a jumbo, shaggy sheepdog passed on a leash, they were flabbergasted why a farm animal was being kept trapped in the middle of a city.

At a major television show in the USA, the sound engineer took it upon himself to "tune" Adrien's guitar. It's hard

Adrien remains one
of the great living
roots songwriters
in any language.

to imagine such liberties being taken with Keith Richards's ax, and if attempted certainly a buff roadie would've taken down the person responsible, without charges ever being pressed. Instead, Adrien returned quizzically to his guitar each time this happened, frowning while plucking the strings until he'd retuned the instrument to where he wanted it to be. This cross-cultural, aesthetic tug-of-war played out repeatedly until the actual taping began.

To actualize full inclusion and diversity we must celebrate the entire continuum of sound, not just the "proper" pitches that have been enshrined. Extraordinary artists do just that, accentuating neglected notes and cadence.

Far from divas, in 2023 the Good Ones likely became the first group in history to return from a world tour and have to walk seventeen hilly miles home in the dark through sketchy neighborhoods while carrying their gear—a way to save some of the money they'd made. Still, they didn't complain. I only learned of it secondhand.

When people use the word "poor" or broke in the USA, they rarely have had to choose between feeding one's family or sending a child to school. If you're ever trying to distinguish economic class anywhere in the world, look down—at a person's shoes . . . and if they have them at all.

My wife Marilena's parents had both lived in rural Africa, so their family later being forced to squat in a factory without running water or electricity for a year in Italy were not unfamiliar. It was a return to normalcy.

American rapper J. Cole may do a vanity fly-by to play professional basketball for the Rwandan team in their shiny new auditorium, but outside the city, the Good Ones still live with dirt floors and sans running water or electricity.

Today, the populace that is routinely rendered invisible in global media are the rural poor. Notwithstanding trends toward urbanization, around half of the world's population continues to reside rurally. The reality is that figure is

Janvier repurposes a hoe from Adrien's farm.

higher since so many rural people are undocumented, as is the case for numerous artists we've worked with who are without birth certificates or known birthdates. In Rwanda, the percentage living rurally stands at 83 percent, a fact that is overshadowed by the development and economic growth in the capital, Kigali.

Yet the foundations of virtually all popular music—gospel, blues, tango, jazz, country, reggae—would not exist were it not for rural musicians. An Afrobeat star from Lagos or an Amapiano performer from Johannesburg often have more in common with residents of high-end London or Manhattan than they do the majority of their own countrymen.

Not coincidentally, the recent global music success stories have come from some of the world's most powerful nations, such as K-pop from Korea (the tenth-largest economy in the world) and Afrobeat from Nigeria (the largest economy in Africa and the most populous nation).

Limitations do not inevitably inhibit creativity though. In many cases, they liberate it. Materials shape as well as are shaped by artists. The history of architecture follows the development of new building materials—concrete led to greater geometric experimentation than had been possible with stone and brick buildings. Nonetheless, some of the most stunning structures remain those that were built hundreds of years before these technological innovations, back when finishing a cathedral or palace was a multigenerational affair.

The history of popular music was shaped by the electric guitar. But the electric guitar itself was shaped by Django Reinhardt (who could only play with two of the fingers on his left hand and was an influence on Wes Montgomery, Chet Atkins, and Willie Nelson) and another guitarist who'd lost fingers in an accident—Tony Iommi of Black Sabbath. In addition to Django having lost use of the third and fourth fingers of his fretting hand, he also required a cane to walk following his burn injuries.

But none of the Good Ones' deprivations are what make them a stellar band. They excel not because of these factors, but in spite of them. Janvier and Adrien's voices entwine familiarly as only those that have sung a lifetime together can—echoing legendary vocal groups like the Everly Brothers, Jackson 5, Carter Family, and the Staple Singers. One of the most striking aspects of the Good Ones' close harmonies is how often their voices dovetail, swapping positions high and low in a way that blurs who's singing which part. Perceptually, their voices become one.

Yet the group carry the burden shared by so many "foreign" language artists: that of being treated as a novelty.

A veteran American critic listed the Good Ones' previous album as one of the year's best. But he dismissed the new record due to having already "covered Rwanda," as if a nation of over thirteen million people is undeserving of being represented more than once. At last count, this writer's publication had published eight separate pieces about Harry Styles's newest album.

Relatedly, many critics have posited that Stromae is a Rwandan artist and attempted to compare his and the Good Ones' music. It is true that Stromae's father was Rwandan, but as wonderful as Stromae's music is, he is Belgian and sings in French, not Kinyarwanda (although he is also reportedly fluent in Flemish). Belgium is one of the world's richest nations, and Stromae attended an elite boarding school. Equating the Good Ones and Stromae is no less misguided than claiming that the California-centric arena rockers Van Halen were "Indonesian artists" due to the Van Halen brothers' mother having been born there.

"I speak fluent French, but I refuse to ever speak it again." These are the words of a family friend from Rwanda that bear the bitterness still found toward Belgian and French colonialism's contributions to the Rwandan genocides which claimed the lives of our friend's entire family.

In Rwanda, there exists a generational linguistic divide. Following the 1994 genocide, the former colonial language of French was officially replaced by English. Therefore, the age of Rwandan citizens can largely be determined by which of the two languages they can speak.

But due to limited access to schools, many rural Rwandan citizens like the Good Ones never received the benefit of the massive linguistic reach of English *or* French. Instead, they only spoke Kinyarwanda before the genocide and continue to do so in the new era.

Yet, if the Good Ones' primary writer, Adrien, sang in English, sported tattoos and a biker chain, and hailed from Brooklyn, Silverlake, or East Nashville, he'd routinely be hailed as a new Dylan. Instead, the group are consistently othered to the "world music" pile and their music's acoustic elements mistaken as "traditional" rather than the highly personal and bespoke songs that they are. Virtually no one has ever attempted to claim that Elliott Smith, Joni Mitchell, or Leonard Cohen are traditional artists simply because they've traded in acoustic sounds.

I am convinced that the Good Ones are the Nick Drake (or Big Star) of global music—their songs predestined to gain a larger audience decades after their music has been released.

With an estimated half million songs uploaded to Spotify weekly and 90 percent of streaming activity being devoted to the 1 percent superstar artists (Drake, Justin Bieber, Taylor Swift, et al.), most people paradoxically listen to fewer voices in the digital era—the exact historical juncture where it's possible to access wider diversity than ever before.

Whatever the widespread aspirational hype around connectivity and cultural boundaries collapsing, out of the Top 100 best-selling albums of 2021 in the USA, thirteen

The Good Ones'
accompanying
member, Mahoro—
whose name means
"peace"—tends
toward silence except
when singing.

were from artists that are long deceased. Another fifteen were records released thirty years or more before including one that debuted in 1959. One quarter of these top sellers' origins are as corporately groomed child stars, four of whom were Disney protégés. Not unrelatedly, three corporations (Universal, Sony, Warner) now distribute around 75 percent or more of the recorded music on earth.

Seminal rapper Gil Scott-Heron claimed in 1970 that "the revolution will not be televised." But when it comes to modern media, the neoliberal revolution is *all* that is televised—24/7 we are bombarded with the capitalistic hijacking of popular music's origins as a bullhorn for the common man.

My and Marilena's endeavors are money-losing labors of love. Rather than a cultural conspiracy, the primary reason that audiences do not hear more diverse international voices is that there is zero money it. Were there, the market would be flooded with music from every corner. Such is capitalism. More than immoral, it is an amoral system, callously following wherever profits lead.

The primary difference between Black and white culture is that Black culture developed survival mechanisms to endure and transcend oppression. White survival strategies, instead, have largely been based *on* oppression.

The records we undertake are never about showing "what 'these people' can do," but instead honoring what an individual *person* has done.

When I see our daughter connect with children her age—as she first did with Adrien's youngest daughter Liliane at age three—and run laughing hand in hand, this is not an illusion of friendship. It is an illustration of how things could be if the barriers between people were lessened and the gross inequities righted. The kids already know—difference is not something to be feared but celebrated.

Emotional injuries settle down deep like fossil fuel. But unlike crude oil, they're not a source of energy. Instead, they drain.

Toward the end of the Rwanda trip, we visited Marilena's mother's remote hilltop village, where her family's hut was burned to the ground and her family members raped and killed. Only Marilena's mother was spared due to her young age and physical disability that requires using a leg brace and crutch.

Rwanda is a landlocked country and is the most densely populated nation in mainland Africa. Though Marilena's mother's village is only around fifty miles away from Adrien's farm, the roads are so porous, steep, and curvy that it took more than four hours to reach there. Adrien had never been to the lake and asked what the "bits of land" were. It took a few rounds to decipher the question. Though, he'd traveled to London and seen the Pacific, Adrien had never beheld an island.

Before heading out, Adrien serenaded the locals with a few tunes and after a single performance of "Columbia River Flowers," the crowd was already singing the hook as we departed.

Lifetimes are contained in his voice. Often, he seems to grow more haunted over the course of a song.

I failed the men. Though maybe not as much as many of their fellow countrymen had, still I failed them. When Adrien recently wrote a song declaring me his best friend, I was shaken. In the face of nearly unbridgeable inequality, my modest efforts have proven outmatched.

Every time I turn on a tap and water arrives on demand, I see their faces and am reminded of the daily scrabble for clean water—their having to carry buckets long distances.

I can't shake witnessing a preteen girl on Ukerewe Island balancing on her head a plastic jug of water nearly half as tall as she, her face and chest drenched in spillage, sweat and strain. The injustice is irreconcilable.

The final Good Ones album concludes with the epic, seven-minute dirge "Love Can Lead the Way," a hard-earned lesson for them. If these two men—who've battled poverty their entire lives, after already having survived not one, but two genocides—can embrace love as a path forward, that can't but be something we should all ponder more closely.

Surely, there must a better way.

Third World in the New World

Who Said You Can't Go Home Again?

I circled these streets for hours
hoping they'd give up names,
but the closest I came was a homeless man screaming,
"It's not me who's insane."

In San Francisco the tampons were under lock and key—along with tubes of toothpaste tethered and treasured.

The vandalism and shoplifting ran so rampant that a pharmacy manager had to be summoned to open plastic containers for even the most mundane items.

Sundries were protected, but the people were not—housed outside in cardboard boxes and doorways.

The demarcated blocks and zones designated for those deemed disposable remain unchanged from when I was growing up in the Bay Area. Only the cast is ever-rotating and replenished by capitalism's grind, the same roles perpetually played.

We were recently in New York following a sitcom star's death. By chance, we passed crowds lined up to pile tens of thousands of dollars of flowers along with handwritten cards at the doorstep of his fictional character's house—one which was only a photographed facade whose interior was never used. Meanwhile, around every neighboring corner from this outpouring, people unhoused slept shivering on sidewalks. Too often, love is a resource selectively wasted, excess care squandered that could've been repurposed and channeled more constructively. But it's so much easier and less threatening emotionally to lavish affections toward those that are distant and imaginary—cases where there is little risk and zero reciprocity.

I attended defunded public schools where the older homeowners, whose children were grown, no longer wanted to pay taxes for the education of their community—a weakening of the social contract and withdrawal into short-sighted self-interest. Reverse Robin Hoods, they took from the poor(er) to give to the rich(est). You'd have to travel another hour northeast out along the Delta marshlands to recreate what my hometown was then—a working-class settling, agricultural land still in transition, beset by prefab homes. The frog colonies out back croaked their warnings nightly.

The gentry redevelop neighborhoods like shaking out blankets and wringing out rags, forcing ever more people onto the streets.

Nowhere in the world that I've been is more "Third World" than here. Blocks from billionaires and the offices of the richest man on earth, a de facto, unstaffed, open-air psych ward runs amok. Many rural families globally have only a hole in the ground to shit in, but here people have *nowhere* at all, denied the most basic of dignities.

There are no "homeless people," only people without a "home."

EPILOGUE

Stars and Scars

When Did We Stop Rooting for the Underdogs?

In San Francisco, I entered a 100 percent organic café where every ingredient was measured and graded. But conspicuously, overhead they played the most synthetic of pop music with zero acoustic instrumentation or audibly unmanipulated voices. It was music created without once living on air.

At a nearby downtown hotel, tech workers twiddled with their phones as they sat in the lobby and salsa music played overhead. They tapped their feet, but not in time to the music. Instead, they were out of sync, movement driven by agitation, oblivious to the rhythms around them. This is a diagnostic hallmark of cultural soul sickness: people moving disjointedly with others in their proximity, even when music is present.

Then on the subway train home, a young woman watched a "slow-cooking" show, played back at double-speed. That same day, a defanged "London Calling" cover beckoned overhead in a café, a manifesto metabolized to muzak—yet another vitriolic song domesticated and eviscerated in service of vacuous consumption. A few months later, I exited one Siena shop—a city with over one thousand years of history and where seventeen microneighborhoods fly separate flags—only to hours later enter a café down the street that was playing the exact same Rolling Stones tune (aptly, "Sympathy for the Devil"). In both cases, the staff playing the music were decades from being born when the song was originally recorded.

In culture there are the pioneers, settlers, and gentrifiers. Dismayingly, most pop performers are the latter. Commercialized personalities are driven by ambition, whereas truer artists are moved emotionally to create.

Corporations have recently spent billions to gobble up celebrity song catalogs, proof that the overlords want our future to sound very much like our past. Additionally, they've launched legal campaigns to strangle creativity further with lawsuits attempting to copyright basic chord progressions—ones that have been shared for centuries and constitute the DNA of folk music. These megacorps have even successfully sued for songs allegedly copying "feel."

It should not be dismissed that musicians would regale arrivals at concentration camps with traditional songs—a false reception, a sedation before administering death. Giving lip service to "diversity," but investing energy in superstars is a contradiction.

Only three nations (out of the more than two hundred countries on earth) export more music than they import—the USA, UK, and Sweden. And almost all of that "Swedish" music is actually in English. Think ABBA and Avicii.

Those who most avidly espouse economic Darwinism, have ironically almost always gained through *un*natural selection—nepotism and the transfer of generational affluence and privilege.

Commercial music is all climax, all the time—an immediate gratification, journeyless state of stasis.

But time is one of our mightiest existential gifts. More than aging us, time's passage allows us to heal—both physically and emotionally. Music is the art form that decorates and demarcates this passage, unfolding across seconds and minutes rather than being irreversibly fixed to an instant.

Far from subtle, corporations are now "programming" us with music, and it is often artificial intelligence doing the honors—studying what music makes us shop more impulsively or move along hurriedly or linger.

I love listening to naked voices—the original instrument unadorned, the tangle of its timbre and grain. A solo voice is the most intimate of instruments. Auto-Tune instead is like doping for singers—a mockery of the art, a cheating of the competition.

The loftiest use of headphones is not to block out sound, but to learn to listen more carefully when we *don't* have them on. I would rather behold a haphazard goatherd bell orchestra than a renowned symphony, for the unplanned will never happen again.

Pop stars today have become largely visual artists—their music almost incidental, an afterthought. A soundtrack for their image. Propped-up by the EpiPen injection of half-naked, tokenized dance troupes, pumped-fist gestures, face tats, misplaced scowls and growls, pyrotechnic light shows, and vacant, Me First exclamations, the intensity is everywhere but in the milquetoast music.

With advancing technology, the music-making process itself has also become increasingly visual due to the various graphic meters available to view sonic measurements. To close our eyes and fully attend to sound is the fullest protest against this primacy of eye over ear. The physical world before us only appears mute if we do not listen.

Most media content today is dishonest—technologically realized simulations or corrections hyped as superhuman performance, undermining music's magical ability to help us find emotional commonality beneath the superficial differences that divide us.

Cobbling together attributable influences is just another form of shopping—a consumeristic act: "Does this 'punk' sound or stance look good on me?"

Pop stars play their identity rather than an instrument. Their expertise is in performing a role, their life spent striking poses. Thus, unable to play the guitar, they break it—postures practiced rather than ability earned. Monsters of mediocrity, they are contaminated by industrial ideation and transactional motives. And it is their music's very illegibility and middling that has paved the way for Artificial Intelligence art and their own obsolescence.

When a famous rapper recently threw her microphone at an unruly audience member, the tantrum unveiled her masquerade—the prerecording of her voice that she'd been pantomiming to continued blasting from the PA. Technology has spawned a new generation of Milli Vanillis.

That music has fully become a commodity that can be possessed is rarely clearer than when people exclaim, "That's my jam," as the first few notes of a favorite song come on.

Whenever I see Afrobeats stars posing with their stable of Lamborghinis and Bentleys, I'm puzzled how this can be mistaken for full inclusion or representation, and not just a retooled manifestation of hypercapitalism's status quo.

More than genres dissolving, music across the board is being homogenized by technology and globalization.

A journalist recently asked me if we were going to a certain country because they were known for music. But our motivation is exactly the opposite. The places most worthy of visiting are those whose musicality has been denied rather than valorized internationally.

I've been to Memphis more than once, but never to Graceland. I could give a rat's ass where lived a King.

Too much art now is context driven. But the most durable art *is* the context. The music stands as evidence to the back story. That story's depths can be sensed and retraced backward from there, if desired. But the music itself bypasses all ideation and reaches straight to the heart—blind taste tests of sound.

Instead when driven by hype machines, music has often been made an accessory, all but tacked on to context and identity.

People want to be heard. They want to be seen. They want to be known.

Stars instead want to be worshipped—revealing their soul (or, most frequently, lack thereof).

Righting inequity is about creating opportunities, not rigging the race. You can be from Cameroon and still suck. You can suck from any place on earth (and more aspiring "artists" globally do than don't). Any individual stops being a genius the minute they start thinking they are one.

Revealingly, even at a "world music" conference, with one of the most famous music producers and ethnomusic-ologists in the world present, not a soul could name as much as a single artists from most nations on earth—even ones that they'd "been to."

I've never subscribed to a fair world. There is too much graphic evidence to the contrary. But that does not absolve us from hoping and fighting for a slightly more just one.

We must challenge invisibility at every turn,

So, we stand back taking potshots with our little pea-shooter—a speck amid mass media's cyclone.

Rather than thousands of distracted "likes," a single person loving a voice is the aim—inspiring a listener to make room for the music to take root deep within their soul.

(The day before the final edited copy of this book was due, I spoke at a conference here in Italy and an older couple came up afterwards.

The wife told me how she'd never heard her husband sing because when he was a child a teacher had convinced him that he was tone deaf. And in all their years, he'd refused to ever dance with her.

But when in the kitchen by himself and a Malawi Mouse Boys' song plays, she said he loosens and wakens, moving to the music.

That story alone makes it all worthwhile.)

Six Simple Daily Practices to Reclaim Your Immediate Environment

1. Close your eyes for at least sixty seconds and listen to sound alone.
2. Animate silent objects such as walls or pans by striking or rubbing them and concentrate on their "voices" for a few seconds—liberating sound from seemingly mute objects.
     Make them speak.
3. Create and repeat one basic and brief rhythmic or melodic structure with just your voice or body.
4. Force yourself to listen to at least one new song a day that you don't like or is sung in a language you don't understand. Actively open yourself to difference.
5. Try to be a tourist toward your own life, to look at or touch the familiar as if for the first time. For a few seconds daily, stop and focus on at least one "known" element, identifying something previously unnoticed or forgotten about it.

---

6. Any time you are at an independently owned business and they are playing corporate music, confront the inconsistency. Kindly suggest that they consider featuring artists as bespoke as their own enterprise, reflecting that scale and model—localized, singular, and ideally in diverse languages.

Brennan recording in Kosovo.

The author diligently preparing for life as a failed musician.

About the Author

Ian Brennan is a Grammy-winning music producer who has also produced three other Grammy-nominated albums. He is the author of nine previous books and has worked with the likes of Fugazi, Merle Haggard, Tinariwen, John Waters, and Green Day, among others. His work with international artists such as the Zomba Prison Project, Tanzania Albinism Collective, Ustad Saami, and Khmer Rouge Survivors, has been featured on the front page of the *New York Times,* the BBC, PBS, NPR, and on an Emmy-winning segment for the television program *60 Minutes* with Anderson Cooper reporting.

He also has taught violence prevention and conflict resolution around the world since 1993 for such prestigious organizations as UC Berkeley, Bellevue Hospital (NYC), the Betty Ford Clinic, and the National Accademia of Science (Rome), and he's spoken about music at the University of London, The New School (NYC), the Smithsonian Institution, WOMADelaide (Australia), Ca' Foscari University (Venice), the Society for the Neuroscience of Creativity, the Audio Engineering Society (AES), and Berklee College of Music, among others.

Marilena Umuhoza Delli at work on São Tomé Island.

About the Photographer

Marilena Umuhoza Delli is an Italian Rwandan photographer, author, and filmmaker whose photographic work has been published around the world by VICE, *Libération*, *Corriere della Sera*, *Le Monde*, *Rolling Stone*, and the *Smithsonian*, among others, and she's photographed the covers of more than three dozen international music albums. She has written three Italian-language books about racism and growing up with an immigrant mother in Italy's most redneck region.

She cofounded the first BIPOC-owned antiracism academy in Italy and holds a master's degree in language for international communication, for which she wrote her thesis on African cinema. She regularly speaks and provides antiracism and diversity workshops throughout Italy, Brazil, the US, and UK.

Experimental and classical percussionist **Evelyn Glennie** has released almost fifty albums and collaborated with the likes of Björk, Fred Frith, Bela Fleck, Bobby McFerrin, and filmmaker Danny Boyle. Evelyn became deaf at age twelve and is the only deaf artist known to have ever won a Grammy, which she has done twice. Glennie is the author of two books, *Listen World!* and *Good Vibrations: My Autobiography*. In 2004, she was the subject of the critically acclaimed documentary *Touch the Sound*. Her stated mission is to try to help "teach the world to listen."

ABOUT PM PRESS

PM Press is an independent, radical publisher of critically necessary books for our tumultuous times. Our aim is to deliver bold political ideas and vital stories to all walks of life and arm the dreamers to demand the impossible. Founded in 2007 by a small group of people with decades of publishing, media, and organizing experience, we have sold millions of copies of our books, most often one at a time, face to face. We're old enough to know what we're doing and young enough to know what's at stake. Join us to create a better world.

PM Press
PO Box 23912
Oakland, CA 94623
www.pmpress.org

PM Press in Europe
europe@pmpress.org
www.pmpress.org.uk

FRIENDS OF PM PRESS

These are indisputably momentous times—the financial system is melting down globally and the Empire is stumbling. Now more than ever there is a vital need for radical ideas.

In the many years since its founding—and on a mere shoestring—PM Press has risen to the formidable challenge of publishing and distributing knowledge and entertainment for the struggles ahead. With hundreds of releases to date, we have published an impressive and stimulating array of literature, art, music, politics, and culture. Using every available medium, we've succeeded in connecting those hungry for ideas and information to those putting them into practice.

Friends of PM allows you to directly help impact, amplify, and revitalize the discourse and actions of radical writers, filmmakers, and artists. It provides us with a stable foundation from which we can build upon our early successes and provides a much-needed subsidy for the materials that can't necessarily pay their own way. You can help make that happen—and receive every new title automatically delivered to your door once a month—by joining as a Friend of PM Press. And, we'll throw in a free T-shirt when you sign up.

Here are your options:

- **$30 a month** Get all books and pamphlets plus a 50% discount on all webstore purchases

- **$40 a month** Get all PM Press releases (including CDs and DVDs) plus a 50% discount on all webstore purchases

- **$100 a month** Superstar—Everything plus PM merchandise, free downloads, and a 50% discount on all webstore purchases

For those who can't afford $30 or more a month, we have **Sustainer Rates** at $15, $10 and $5. Sustainers get a free PM Press T-shirt and a 50% discount on all purchases from our website.

Your Visa or Mastercard will be billed once a month, until you tell us to stop. Or until our efforts succeed in bringing the revolution around. Or the financial meltdown of Capital makes plastic redundant. Whichever comes first.

Silenced by Sound: The Music Meritocracy Myth

Ian Brennan
with a Foreword by Tunde
Adebimpe

ISBN: 978-1-62963-703-7
$20.00   256 pages

Popular culture has woven itself into the social
fabric of our lives, penetrating people's homes
and haunting their psyches through images and earworm hooks. Justice,
at most levels, is something the average citizen may have little influence
upon, leaving us feeling helpless and complacent. But pop music is a
neglected arena where concrete change can occur—by exercising active
and thoughtful choices to reject the low-hanging, omnipresent corporate
fruit, we begin to rebalance the world, one engaged listener at a time.

Silenced by Sound: The Music Meritocracy Myth is a powerful exploration
of the challenges facing art, music, and media in the digital era. With his
fifth book, producer, activist, and author Ian Brennan delves deep into his
personal story to address the inequity of distribution in the arts globally.
Brennan challenges music industry tycoons by skillfully demonstrating
that there are millions of talented people around the world far more
gifted than the superstars for whom billions of dollars are spent to
promote the delusion that they have been blessed with unique genius.

We are invited to accompany the author on his travels, finding and
recording music from some of the world's most marginalized peoples.
In the breathtaking range of this book, our preconceived notions of art
are challenged by musicians from South Sudan to Kosovo, as Brennan
lucidly details his experiences recording music by the Tanzania Albinism
Collective, the Zomba Prison Project, a "witch camp" in Ghana, the
Vietnamese war veterans of Hanoi Masters, the Malawi Mouse Boys,
the Canary Island whistlers, genocide survivors in both Cambodia and
Rwanda, and more.

Silenced by Sound is defined by muscular, terse, and poetic verse, and
a nonlinear format rife with how-to tips and anecdotes. The narrative
is driven and made corporeal via the author's ongoing field-recording
chronicles, his memoir-like reveries, and the striking photographs that
accompany these projects.

After reading it, you'll never hear quite the same again.

Muse-Sick: a music manifesto in fifty-nine notes

Ian Brennan with a Foreword by John Waters

ISBN: 978-1-62963-909-3
$14.95   128 pages

Grammy-winning music producer Ian Brennan's seventh book, *Muse-Sick*, is a primer on how mass production and commercialization have corrupted the arts. Broken down into a series of core points and action plans, it expands upon Brennan's previous music missives, *Silenced by Sound: The Music Meritocracy Myth and How Music Dies (or Lives)*.

Popular culture has woven itself into the social fabric of our lives through images and earworm hooks. Justice, at most levels, is something one may have little influence upon, leaving us feeling helpless and complacent. But pop music is a neglected arena where concrete change can occur. By exercising active and thoughtful choices to reject the low-hanging, omnipresent commercialized and prepackaged fruit, we begin to rebalance the world, one engaged listener at a time.

In fifty-nine clear and concise points, Brennan reveals how corporate media has constricted local cultures and individual creativity, leading to a lack of diversity within "diversity." *Muse-Sick*'s narrative portions are driven and made corporeal via the author's ongoing field-recording chronicles of places including Comoros, Kosovo, Pakistan, and Rwanda, with disparate groups such as the Sheltered Workshop Singers, brought to life by Marilena Umuhoza Delli's striking photographs.

"*Ian Brennan's* Muse-Sick *is a passionate, thought-provoking chronicle of traveling beyond the mainstream to listen to unheard music created by the unsung.*"
—Maureen Mahon, NYU, author of *Right to Rock: The Black Rock Coalition and the Cultural Politics of Race and Black Diamond Queens*

"*We can never hear enough of the fresh, conscientious perspective of Ian Brennan. His words gives voice to people who have been silenced.*"
—Booker T. Jones, frontman of Booker T. and the M.G.'s and winner of the Grammy Lifetime Achievement Award

Where Are the Elephants?

Leon Rosselson

ISBN: 978-1-62963-973-4
$16.95   184 pages

Fierce and funny, this memoir in essay and song is full of wonderful tales of art and protest. Leon Rosselson's *Where Are the Elephants?* is a rare behind the scenes look at the life and times of one of England's foremost folksingers. This clear-eyed portrait of an activist who never gave up and whose talent, wit, and verve brought the world into finer focus provides a model for a whole new generation of radicals. Fans will love revisiting the lyrics from his hits—and behind the scenes glimpses of the stories and events that inspired his songs, but Rosselson's story of growing from a red diaper baby into a modern troubadour up against the barricades is a tale for the ages.

"*In many ways, Leon Rosselson is the embodiment of the original ideals of punk rock. His hair isn't spiky, but his music is, using fearless wit and political integrity to highlight the hypocrisies of those in power. Alone among the great British songwriters of the past sixty years, Leon has sought to make art that stays true to Karl Marx's demand that we should concern ourselves with the ruthless criticism of all that exists.*"
—Billy Bragg

"*Rosselson remains fearless. He provides something that the world is in dire need of currently—dissent that seeks dialogue versus greater division and disconnection.*"
—Ian Brennan, Grammy-winning music producer and author, *Silenced by Sound* and *Muse-Sick: a music manifesto in fifty-nine notes*

"*His songs are teeming with colorful characters, wonderfully descriptive passages and witty observations.*"
—*Washington Post*

"*Proof that the art of songwriting is not dead. Occasionally, acid flows from his pen but always the end-product is thoughtful, witty and provocative.*"
—Sheffield Telegraph

"*His songs are fierce, funny, cynical, outraged, blasphemous, challenging and anarchic. And the tunes are good too.*"
—*Guardian*

The Fascist Groove Thing: A History of Thatcher's Britain in 21 Mixtapes

Hugh Hodges with a Preface by Dick Lucas and a Foreword by Boff Whalley

ISBN: 978-162-963-884-3
$22.95   384 pages

This is the late 1970s and '80s as explained through the urgent and still-relevant songs of the Clash, the Specials, the Au Pairs, the Style Council, the Pet Shop Boys, and nearly four hundred other bands and solo artists. Each chapter presents a mixtape (or playlist) of songs related to an alarming feature of Thatcher's Britain, followed by an analysis of the dialogue these artists created with the Thatcherite vision of British society. "Tell us the truth," Sham 69 demanded, and pop music, however improbably, did. It's a furious and sardonic account of dark times when pop music raised a dissenting fist against Thatcher's fascist groove thing and made a glorious, boredom-smashing noise. Bookended with contributions by Dick Lucas and Boff Whalley as well as an annotated discography, *The Fascist Groove Thing* presents an original and polemical account of the era.

"*It's not often that reading history books works best with a soundtrack playing simultaneously, but Hugh Hodges has succeeded in evoking both the noises and the feel of a tumultuous 1980s. Proving that pop music is the historian's friend, he has here recovered those who help us best make sense of a scary, precarious, and exciting world.*"
—Matthew Worley, author of *No Future: Punk, Politics and British Youth Culture, 1976–1984*

"*Those who think the 1980s were camp and fun clearly didn't live them. The Thatcher/Reagan era was grim as fuck. This tells the real story from the underground.*"
—Ian Brennan, author of *Muse-Sick* and *Silenced by Sound*

"*Very interesting and timely indeed.*"
—Anne Clark, spoken-word poet, *The Smallest Act of Kindness*

If It Sounds Good, It Is Good: Seeking Subversion, Transcendence, and Solace in America's Music

Richard Manning with a Foreword by Rick Bass

ISBN: 978-1-62963-792-1
$26.95   320 pages

Music is fundamental to human existence, a cultural universal among all humans for all times. It is embedded in our evolution, encoded in our DNA, which is to say, essential to our survival. Academics in a variety of disciplines have considered this idea to devise explanations that Richard Manning, a lifelong journalist, finds hollow, arcane, incomplete, ivory-towered, and just plain wrong. He approaches the question from a wholly different angle, using his own guitar and banjo as instruments of discovery. In the process, he finds himself dancing in celebration of music rough and rowdy.

American roots music is not a product of an elite leisure class, as some academics contend, but of explosive creativity among slaves, hillbillies, field hands, drunks, slackers, and hucksters. Yet these people—poor, working people—built the foundations of jazz, gospel, blues, bluegrass, rock 'n' roll, and country music, an unparalleled burst of invention. This is the counterfactual to the academics' story. This is what tells us music is essential, but by pulling this thread, Manning takes us down a long, strange path, following music to deeper understandings of racism, slavery, inequality, meditation, addiction, the science of our brains, and ultimately to an enticing glimpse of pure religion.

Use this book to follow where his guitar leads. Ultimately it sings the American body, electric.

"Richard Manning is the most significant social critic in the northern Rockies. We're fortunate to have Dick Manning as he continues his demands for fairness while casting light on our future."
—William Kittredge, author of *The Last Best Place: A Montana Anthology* and *The Next Rodeo: New and Selected Essays*

"Richard Manning's work has always been something special, distinguished by its intense passion and its penetrating insights."
—George Black, author of *Empire of Shadows: The Epic Story of Yellowstone*